nursery crafts

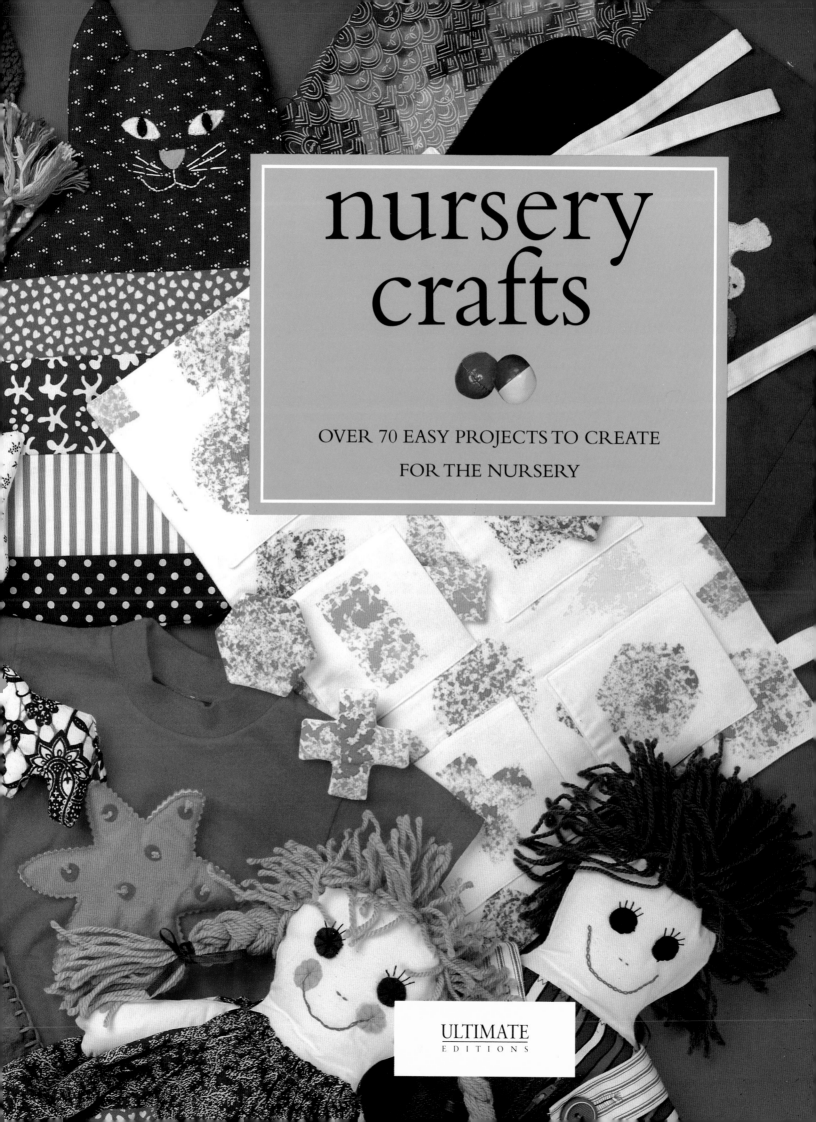

nursery crafts

OVER 70 EASY PROJECTS TO CREATE

FOR THE NURSERY

ULTIMATE
EDITIONS

First published in 1995 by Ultimate Editions

© 1995 Anness Publishing Limited

Ultimate Editions is an imprint of
Anness Publishing Limited
1 Boundary Row Studios
London SE1 8HP

Distributed in Australia by Reed Editions

This edition distributed in Canada by
Book Express, an imprint of
Raincoast Book Distribution Limited

ISBN 1-86035-075-5

Editorial Director: Joanna Lorenz
Project Editor: Penelope Cream
Editor: Jane Royston
Designers: Kit and David Johnson
Photographer: Mark Gatehouse
Illustrators: John Hutchinson and
Maggie Raynor

Previously published as part of a larger
compendium *Baby Gifts*.

Designs in this book remain the copyright
of the publisher and may not be made
for re-sale

Printed by Star Standard
Industries (Pte.) Ltd, Singapore
Typeset by MC Typeset Limited

Threadbear, the little teddy bear featured
in some of the pictures, appears by kind
permission of his owner Mick Inkpen and
his publishers Hodder & Stoughton,
Euston Road, London NW1 3BH

HOW TO USE THE MEASUREMENTS

All craftspeople have their own way of working and feel most comfortable calculating in their preferred measurements. So, where applicable, the option of metric, imperial and cup measures are given. The golden rule is to choose only one set of measurements and to stick with it consistently throughout each project to ensure accurate results.

PUBLISHER'S NOTE

Crafts and hobbies are great fun to learn and can fill many hours of rewarding leisure time, but some special points should be remembered for safety, particularly when making gifts for babies and young children.

■ Always be aware of the materials you are using; use natural fabrics such as cotton and felt wherever possible, and make sure all sewing is strong and firm: double seam or stitch if in any doubt.

■ Always choose non-toxic materials, especially paints, glue and varnishes. Wood must always be smooth and free from splinters and sharp corners. Only use non-toxic flame retardant polyester stuffing or batting to fill soft toys.

■ Any gift with small pieces should not be given to young babies: they are experts at fitting even the most unlikely things into their mouths. Always pull with all your strength on buttons, safety eyes and other parts attached to a project: if an adult cannot remove them, a baby will not be able to either.

■ Secure small items such as bells or squeakers within soft toys inside a little fabric bag for extra safety.

■ Finally, make sure you do not leave your craft materials – such as craft knives, small saws, knitting needles, crochet hooks or adhesives – within the reach of young children.

SOME USEFUL TERMS

UK	US
Calico	Cotton fabric
Cast off	Bind off
Chipboard	Particle board
Cotton wool	Absorbent cotton
Double knitting yarn	Sport yarn
Drawing pins	Thumb tacks
Fretsaw	Scroll saw
Icing sugar	Confectioner's sugar
Lawn	Fine cotton
Matt emulsion paint	Flat latex paint
Muslin	Cheesecloth
Palette knife	Spatula
Panel pins	Finishing nails
Plain flour	All-purpose flour
Polystyrene	Styrofoam
PVC plastic	Vinyl plastic
Towelling	Terrycloth
Zip	Zipper

Contents

Batik Quilt

CREATE YOUR OWN SPECIAL QUILT FOR A NEW-BORN BABY

YOU WILL NEED ■ *1.5 m × 60 cm (60 × 24 in) white cotton fabric*
■ *Scissors* ■ *Drawing pins (thumb tacks)* ■ *Wooden frame* ■ *Soft pencil* ■ *Wax pot or*
bain-marie ■ *Wax granules/block* ■ *Wax brush* ■ *Blue, yellow, red and green cold water dyes*
■ *Paintbrushes* ■ *Newspaper or plain paper* ■ *Iron* ■ *Medium-weight wadding (batting)*
■ *Pins* ■ *Needle and thread* ■ *Fabric edging*

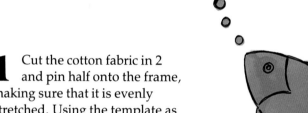

1 Cut the cotton fabric in 2 and pin half onto the frame, making sure that it is evenly stretched. Using the template as a guide, draw the fish design and border onto the material using a soft pencil.

2 Heat the wax, following the manufacturer's instructions if using a wax pot. If heating wax in a bain-marie, check that it is sufficiently hot by testing it on a spare piece of fabric. The wax should soak into the fabric. If the wax seems to lie on the surface, it is not yet hot enough. Paint the wax onto all the areas of the design which are to remain white.

Make up the dyes following the manufacturer's instructions. Paint the dye onto the fabric beginning with the blue border area and using a medium brush. Use a smaller brush to paint the colours of the fish. Some 'bleeding' may occur between colours. Do not worry, as this can add to the attractiveness of the design. Allow to dry naturally.

3 Remove the fabric from the frame. Put some newspaper or plain paper on an ironing board, place the fabric on the paper and place another sheet of paper on top. Iron the fabric with a very hot iron, pressing evenly throughout. The paper will absorb and remove most of the wax. Hand-wash the batiked cloth in lukewarm soapy water to remove any excess dye. Dry clean to remove every trace of wax from the fabric.

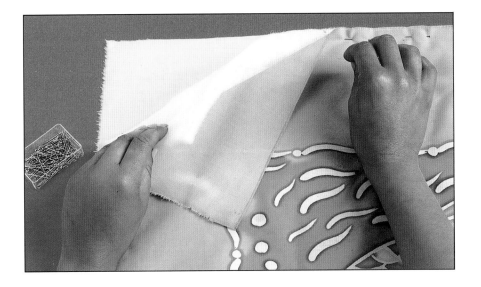

5 Pin around the border design in the centre and tack (baste) again. Pin the edging fabric around the border of the quilt, tack (baste) and sew. Stitch around the centre border design to create the quilted effect.

4 Place the unpainted piece of white fabric onto a clean, even surface. Cut a piece of wadding (batting) to size, position this on the backing and finally place the cover design on top. Carefully pin all the layers together and then tack (baste).

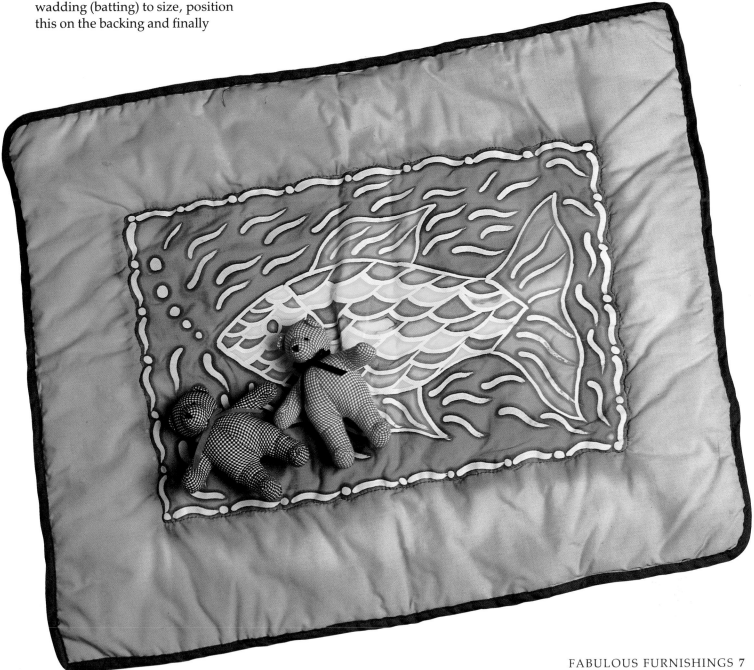

Nursery Curtains

THESE BRIGHT AND CHEERFUL CURTAINS ARE EASY TO MAKE

YOU WILL NEED ■ *Tape measure* ■ *Fabric for curtains* ■ *Scissors*
■ *32 × 90 cm (12½ × 36 in) contrasting fabric for loops* ■ *Pins* ■ *Needle and thread* ■ *46 × 90 cm*
(18¼ × 36 in) contrasting fabric for spikes ■ *Pinking shears* ■ *Curtain pole*

1 Measure your window and cut 2 pieces of fabric for each curtain to fit, allowing for a 2.5 cm (1 in) seam allowance. Cut 6 pieces 32 × 12 cm (12½ × 4¾ in) for the loops. You will need 3 loops for each curtain. To make the loops, fold over each fabric piece lengthwise, pin and sew along the edge, then turn right side out. Cut 6 large triangles for the spikes. Pin and sew them together in pairs, right sides facing. Trim the edges and turn right side out. You will need 3 spikes for each curtain.

2 Trap the loops and spikes inside each front and back piece of curtain, pin, tack (baste) and sew around the edges leaving a gap to turn inside out. Trim edges with pinking shears, turn right side out and sew up the gap.

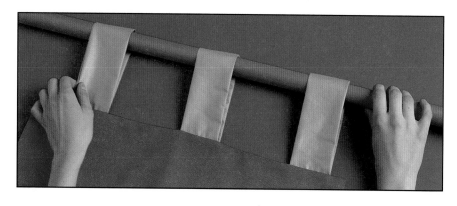

3 Fit the curtains onto the pole before attaching it securely to the wall.

Nursery Pelmet

THIS STRIKING PELMET CO-ORDINATES WELL WITH THE NURSERY CURTAINS

YOU WILL NEED ■ Tape measure ■ Pinking shears ■ 2 pieces of fabric to match the length and sides of your pelmet board ■ Pen ■ Paper ■ Scissors ■ Pins ■ Contrasting fabric for the scalloped trim ■ Needle and thread ■ Velcro ■ Large buttons

1 Measure and cut out 2 fabric pieces to fit the front and sides of the pelmet board. Draw a scallop shape on paper and use it as a template to cut 12 shapes for the 6 scallops. Sew right sides together in pairs leaving the straight side open. Trim and turn right side out.

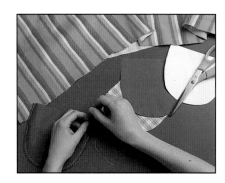

2 Sew a strip of Velcro along the top edge of the back pelmet piece, right side out.

3 Trap the scallop shapes in between the 2 pelmet pieces and sew down both long edges, leaving the ends open to turn right side out.

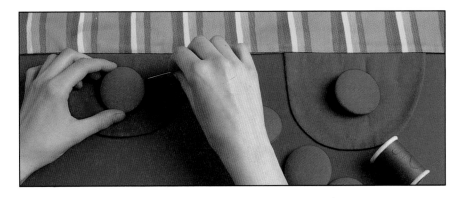

4 Sew the buttons onto the front of the scallop shapes. Sew another strip of Velcro onto the top front edge of the pelmet board and attach the pelmet to the pelmet board.

Tie-dye Sheet

BRIGHTEN UP BEDTIME WITH THIS EYE-CATCHING SHEET

YOU WILL NEED ■ *100 per cent cotton cot (crib) sheet* ■ *String* ■ *Scissors* ■ *Pink and yellow dyes*
■ *2 buckets* ■ *Rubber gloves* ■ *Iron*

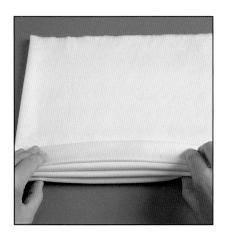

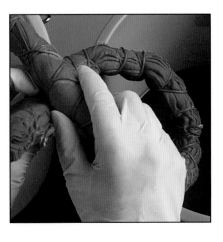

1 Lay the sheet onto a flat surface and fold in half and then into quarters. Fold the sheet up, about 2.5 cm (1 in) at a time, like a concertina, alternately once over, once under, until the whole sheet is folded.

2 Tie string tightly at each end and once in the middle to hold the sheet together. Then in a spiral motion firmly wrap the string all the way down to the end and back again. Fasten in a knot and cut the string.

3 Prepare the dyes in separate buckets, following the manufacturer's instructions, and wearing rubber gloves, immerse the sheet first in the pink dye and then in the yellow.

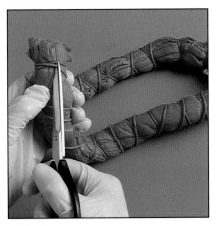

4 Take the sheet out of the dye and rinse under cold water until the dye stops running. Cut the string and open out the sheet. Wash carefully by hand and iron before use. Further dye may come out of the sheet during subsequent laundering, so wash the sheet either by hand, or separately in a warm machine wash.

Patchwork Curtains

A SIMPLE WAY TO CO-ORDINATE NURSERY FURNISHINGS

YOU WILL NEED ■ *Ready-made curtain or a curtain you are making yourself*
■ *Tape measure* ■ *Pencil* ■ *Paper* ■ *Scissors* ■ *Assorted fabrics to match or co-ordinate with the*
curtain ■ *Iron-on interfacing (optional)* ■ *Iron* ■ *Needle and thread* ■ *Pins*

1 This design can be adapted to fit across any curtain as the strip is sewn or appliquéd onto it. On a home-made curtain, do the decorative work before making it up. On a bought curtain, unpick the hem and enough of the lining at the side to allow you to sew the appliquéd strip to the front.

2 Calculate the sizes and number of squares and strips you will need, remembering to add in seam allowances. Using the template as a guide, cut out paper patterns for the flower shapes and cut out all the elements for your work using iron-on interfacing on any flowers cut out in delicate or easily frayed fabric. Join the dividers and light squares first to make the basic strip, with right sides together. Press all the seams open.

3 Appliqué the flower shapes onto the dark squares then tack (baste) the dark squares onto alternate light squares and appliqué them in place. Finish by appliquéing the remaining flower shapes onto the remaining light squares. Turn under the raw edges of the completed strip and tack (baste), then use a decorative stitch to stitch the hem down.

4 Take the completed strip and pin and tack (baste) it to the front of your curtain. Sew it to the front either by hemming or using a decorative stitch. Press firmly. Re-sew any unpicked work on an existing curtain, or continue making up your own new curtain.

Nursery Frieze

MAKE THIS POTATO PRINT FRIEZE AS LONG AS YOU LIKE TO COVER THE WALLS

YOU WILL NEED ■ *Wallpaper lining paper* ■ *Large paintbrush*
■ *Non-toxic acrylic paints* ■ *Kitchen knife* ■ *Large potatoes*

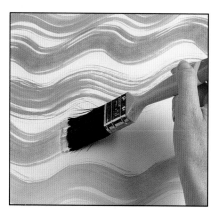

1 Lay out the lining paper and lightly paint in rows of wavy lines in 2 different shades of blue to represent the waves.

2 Using a knife, cut from the potatoes 3 slightly different triangular sail shapes and the 3 hulls for the boats, one for each different colour.

3 Dip the potato shapes into coloured paint and print firmly onto the surface of the paper, positioning them at slightly different angles and spacing them evenly. Leave to dry.

Painted Chair

DECORATE A PLAIN NURSERY CHAIR WITH THIS WOODLAND DESIGN

YOU WILL NEED ■ *Nursery chair* ■ *Sandpaper* ■ *Chalk* ■ *Non-toxic acrylic paints*
■ *Small paintbrush* ■ *Medium paintbrush* ■ *Non-toxic clear acrylic varnish*

1 Lightly rub down the chair with sandpaper. Chalk in the outlines of your design.

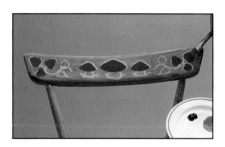

2 Paint in all the base colours with a small paintbrush, red for the strawberries and toadstools, and green for the leaves. Allow the paint to dry.

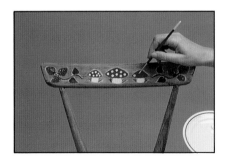

3 Add final details such as the white spots and stalks on the toadstools and the brown flecks on the strawberries.

4 Finally seal the whole chair with a coat of varnish.

FABULOUS FURNISHINGS **13**

Stencilled Toy Box

THIS JOLLY JUGGLER MOTIF WILL BRIGHTEN UP A PLAIN WOODEN TOY BOX

YOU WILL NEED ■ *Pencil* ■ *White paper* ■ *Masking tape* ■ *Sheets of acetate*
■ *Marker pen* ■ *Cutting board* ■ *Craft knife* ■ *Toy box* ■ *Stencil brush* ■ *Non-toxic acrylic paints*
■ *Non-toxic clear acrylic varnish* ■ *Paintbrush*

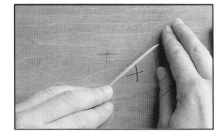

1 Scale up the stencil design from the template onto plain white paper and include 4 position marks. Tape down the acetate onto the drawing and, using the permanent marker pen, draw in the position marks and the outlines of the areas to be stencilled with the first colour.

Take off the acetate and, using a cutting board, cut out the first area of colour with a craft knife. Repeat this process, using a new sheet of acetate for each separate colour, including a sheet for all the juggling balls. Remember to include the position marks.

2 Tape the first colour onto the toy box and mark the position marks onto the box making sure that the final stencil will be correctly positioned.

3 Using the stencil brush, apply the first colour. Repeat with each separate piece of acetate, being careful to line up the position marks accurately each time, until you have finished all the colours. Do each juggling ball as you go along. When the paint is completely dry, seal with a coat of non-toxic varnish.

14

Marine Chest of Drawers

TRANSFORM AN OLD CHEST OF DRAWERS WITH SIMPLE SPONGE EFFECTS

YOU WILL NEED ■ *Chest of drawers* ■ *Sandpaper* ■ *Soft cloth* ■ *Matt white emulsion (flat latex) paint* ■ *Paintbrushes* ■ *Matt peach emulsion (flat latex) paint* ■ *Matt turquoise emulsion (flat latex) paint* ■ *Scissors* ■ *Sponge scourers* ■ *Dishes* ■ *Non-toxic clear acrylic varnish*

1 Prepare a piece of furniture by sanding it to smooth the surface. Then rub it down with a damp cloth to remove any dirt and dust. Next paint on a coat of white emulsion (flat latex) paint to seal the wood. When this is dry apply 2 coats of peach emulsion (flat latex) paint. Mix a little white with the peach emulsion (flat latex) paint to make the pale peach used on the drawers.

2 While the paint is drying, and using the templates as a guide, cut out the fish and starfish from sponge scourers.

3 Pour some white and turquoise emulsion (flat latex) paint into two dishes. Dip the fish-shaped sponge into the white paint, taking care not to overload it, and lightly sponge on to the piece of furniture. When the white paint is dry, repeat the process with the turquoise emulsion (flat latex) paint and the starfish shape until the design is completed.

4 Finally, when the paint is dry, to protect the piece of furniture varnish it all over with 2 coats of acrylic varnish.

Sailing Ship Cabinet

THIS NAUTICAL IDEA WILL BRIGHTEN UP ANY PIECE OF NURSERY FURNITURE

YOU WILL NEED ■ *Sandpaper* ■ *Cabinet or cupboard* ■ *Soft cloth*
■ *Paintbrushes* ■ *Matt white emulsion (flat latex) paint* ■ *Matt blue emulsion (flat latex) paint* ■ *Scissors* ■ *Picture of a ship, photocopied in several sizes* ■ *Rubber-based glue*
■ *Non-toxic acrylic paints* ■ *Non-toxic, clear acrylic varnish* ■ *Oak coloured varnish*

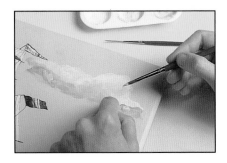

1 Sand your chosen piece of furniture with sandpaper then wipe it with a damp cloth. Paint on a coat of white emulsion (flat latex) paint and allow to dry. Then paint on 2 coats of pale blue emulsion (flat latex), allowing time to dry between coats. Carefully cut out your photocopied images and arrange them on the furniture. Stick them down with rubber-based glue, making sure that they are flat and smooth. Allow to dry for at least 2 hours.

2 Next paint watery washes of acrylic colour onto the photocopied boats to give them depth and make them look realistic. Use plain blue for the sea and yellow ochre for the sails, seams and rigging. Use raw umber for the clouds. Use a mixture of yellow ochre with white for the highlights and raw umber with white for the lowlights, painting in a swirling motion and blending the 2 colours together with your fingers to give added texture.

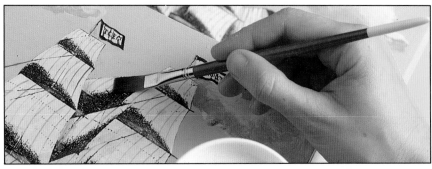

3 Allow the acrylic paints to dry thoroughly. This will take about 2 hours, although you can speed up the process slightly by placing the piece of furniture in a warm (but not too hot) position. When the paints are completely dry, paint a thin coat of clear acrylic varnish over the whole surface with a fairly large brush. This is an important stage, as this varnish will protect the paper from the final varnishing, which requires some rubbing.

4 When the acrylic varnish is dry, paint on the oak coloured varnish taking a small area at a time, and rub off in a circular motion with a clean cloth. Leave some of the stain in some areas to give the piece an aged look. Finish with another coat of the clear varnish.

Starry Pinboard

THIS SIMPLE PINBOARD WILL ADD A BRIGHT SPLASH TO THE NURSERY

YOU WILL NEED ■ *Pinboard* ■ *Felt slightly larger than pinboard* ■ *Rubber-based glue or staple gun* ■ *Scissors* ■ *Self-adhesive coloured felt* ■ *2 picture hooks*

1 Cover the front of the pinboard with the piece of felt and secure it at the back using either a staple gun or glue.

2 Cut out an equal number of star and dot shapes from coloured felt (if you cannot find self-adhesive felt, use rubber-based glue on the reverse of the shapes). Stick the dots in the middle of the star shapes.

3 Arrange the stars over the pinboard and stick down. To secure to the wall attach 2 picture hooks to the back.

Butterfly and Daisy Lampshade

BRING A BREATH OF COUNTRY AIR INTO A BEDROOM WITH THIS PRETTY LAMPSHADE

YOU WILL NEED ■ *Paper- or fabric-covered lampshade with wire support rings* ■ *Pressed daisy flowers* ■ *Tweezers* ■ *Rubber-based glue* ■ *Toothpick* ■ *Scissors* ■ *Paper butterflies* ■ *Iron-on protective laminating film* ■ *Soft cloth* ■ *Heat resistant foam* ■ *Iron* ■ *Strong clear glue*

2 Still using the tweezers, turn each one over and press lightly into position.

4 Laminate the finished design with the iron-on protective laminating film. To do this, cut a piece of film to cover the shade generously, and peel back the first 10 cm (4 in) of the backing paper. Overlap one end by 12 mm (½ in), and gently smooth down the film, peeling off the back paper as you unroll. Make sure that no air bubbles are formed. Use a soft cloth to rub down the film evenly as you work.

1 Carefully peel apart the seam of the lampshade covering and remove from the metal rings. Lay it out and leave under a weight to flatten. Starting at the edges, hold each flower using the tweezers and apply a dot of rubber-based glue to the centre back of each one with a toothpick.

3 Carefully cut out the paper butterflies and stick several of these among the daisies.

5 Cover with a sheet of heat resistant foam, and fix down the protective film by pressing down in sections with an iron at wool heat setting. Trim any excess film, but leave the 12 mm (½ in) overlap at one end, and turn the covering over. Apply a thin line of strong clear glue to the bottom and top edges of the inside of the covering, and glue to the wire rings. Seal the 12 mm (½ in) overlap to finish.

Two-height **C**hair

THIS VERSATILE CHAIR CAN BE USED EITHER WAY UP

YOU WILL NEED ■ Ruler ■ Pencil ■ Tracing paper ■ Masking tape ■ 2 pieces of 30 × 30 cm (12 × 12 in) plywood, 8 mm ($^5/_{16}$ in) thick ■ Clamps ■ Hand drill ■ Fretsaw (scroll saw) ■ Coarse and fine sandpaper ■ 2 plywood side pieces, each 30 × 30 cm (12 × 12 in), 8 mm ($^5/_{16}$ in) thick ■ 1 plywood seat piece, 30 × 32 cm (12 × 12½ in), 8 mm ($^5/_{16}$ in) thick ■ 2 plywood back pieces, 18 × 32 cm (7 × 12½ in) and 12.5 × 32 cm (5 × 12½ in), both 8 mm ($^5/_{16}$ in) thick ■ Craft knife ■ 2 softwood battens, 30 × 4 cm (12 × 1½ in), 2.5 cm (1 in) thick ■ 4 × 5 cm (2 in) brass screws and cups ■ Screwdriver ■ Non-toxic clear acrylic varnish ■ Paintbrush

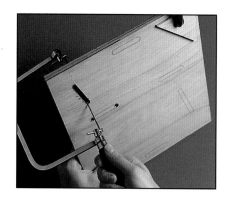

1 Scale up the template onto tracing paper. Attach the paper with masking tape to one of the square pieces of plywood and transfer the design.

2 Clamp both side pieces together. Drill out the ends of the slots with an 8 mm ($^5/_{16}$ in) drill bit and cut out the surplus with a fretsaw (scroll saw). Smooth the edges with sandpaper.

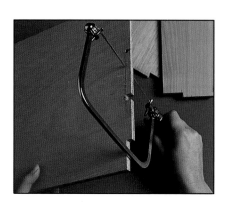

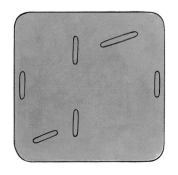

3 In turn, place the seat and the 2 back pieces in position on the slotted sides and mark off the position of the tongues to fit the slots. The tongues should be 1 cm (⅜ in) deep. Cut away the excess wood. Use a craft knife to round the ends of the tongues so that they fit the slots exactly.

4 To complete the chair, assemble the seat and 2 back pieces and then position the 2 softwood battens beneath the front edges of the seat at both heights. Drill the screw through the ends, protecting the screw heads with the screw cups. Finish with 2 coats of varnish.

Braided Mat

A SIMPLE BUT EFFECTIVE MAT USING ODDMENTS OF FABRIC

YOU WILL NEED ■ *Scissors* ■ *Assorted oddments of fabric, torn or cut into long strips about 2 cm (¾ in) wide* ■ *Needle and thread* ■ *Iron*

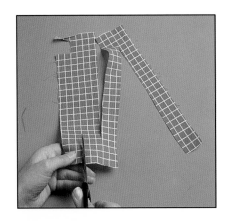

1 Tie 3 strips together, anchor them to a chair or table and braid them fairly tightly. When an individual strip is almost down to its end, add a new one in with it and work the 2 together.

2 Short but wide oddments of fabric can be cut in a zigzag to form a longer piece.

3 Once you have a few metres (yards) of braid, start to make up the mat. Begin by sewing the braid to itself and start to form a spiral, taking the needle over the free end of the braid and catching it to the sewn line. Always work from the same side, which should remain the mat front. Tuck any odd protruding shapes in the strip edges to the back of the mat.

4 When you are happy with the size of your mat, secure the last braid end to the spiral edge. Press the whole mat very firmly to help the shape set in. A very large mat, or one that feels loose, can be backed by sewing it to a heavy cotton fabric.

Laundry Basket

THIS SPRING-FRESH LAUNDRY BASKET IS PERFECT FOR THE NURSERY

YOU WILL NEED ■ *Matt white emulsion (flat latex) paint* ■ *Paintbrushes*
■ *Wicker laundry basket* ■ *Blue and red acrylic paints* ■ *Dishes*

1 Paint the wicker laundry basket with 2 or 3 coats of matt white emulsion (flat latex) paint. Make sure that all the cracks and holes are well covered.

2 Leave until completely dry. Mix on separate dishes a little of the blue and red acrylic paints with white emulsion to make the colours paler. Paint the pale blue and pink onto any details showing on the wicker basket such as the handle on the lid. Remember to make sure that the paints are completely dry before using the basket!

Ribbon Board

A PRETTY WAY TO DISPLAY ANYTHING FROM PHOTOS TO PICTURES

YOU WILL NEED ■ *75 × 75 cm (30 × 30 in) chipboard (particle board), 1.3 cm (½ in) thick* ■ *100 × 100 cm (40 × 40 in) yellow felt* ■ *Staple gun* ■ *Scissors* ■ *1.8 m (2 yd) green ribbon, 1.8 m (2 yd) pink ribbon, 1.8 m (2 yd) red ribbon, 4.8 m (5 yd) blue ribbon, all 1.3 cm (½ in) wide* ■ *Tape measure* ■ *Pins* ■ *50 cm (19½ in) white cord*

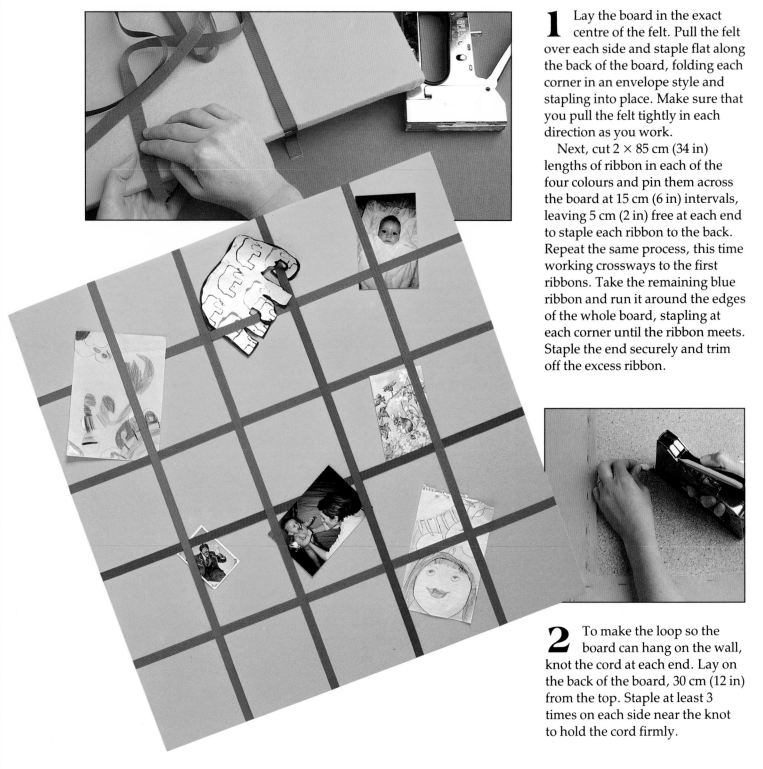

1 Lay the board in the exact centre of the felt. Pull the felt over each side and staple flat along the back of the board, folding each corner in an envelope style and stapling into place. Make sure that you pull the felt tightly in each direction as you work.

Next, cut 2 × 85 cm (34 in) lengths of ribbon in each of the four colours and pin them across the board at 15 cm (6 in) intervals, leaving 5 cm (2 in) free at each end to staple each ribbon to the back. Repeat the same process, this time working crossways to the first ribbons. Take the remaining blue ribbon and run it around the edges of the whole board, stapling at each corner until the ribbon meets. Staple the end securely and trim off the excess ribbon.

2 To make the loop so the board can hang on the wall, knot the cord at each end. Lay on the back of the board, 30 cm (12 in) from the top. Staple at least 3 times on each side near the knot to hold the cord firmly.

Twirling Parrots Mobile

THE MOVEMENT OF THESE TWIRLING PARROTS WILL FASCINATE YOUNG CHILDREN

YOU WILL NEED ■ *Pencil* ■ *Tracing paper* ■ *Thick card* ■ *Scissors* ■ *Poster paints* ■ *Paintbrush*
■ *Coloured ribbon in 3 colours* ■ *Dowelling*

1 Scale up the parrot template to the size required and trace onto thick card. Cut out carefully using scissors. Trace and cut out a total of 3 parrots.

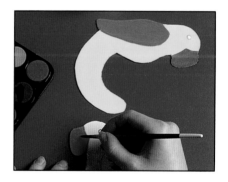

2 Paint the parrots in a variety of bright colours and leave to dry thoroughly.

3 Pierce a small hole in the back of each parrot's neck and thread through a piece of coloured ribbon. Knot the end to secure and tie the other end to the dowelling. Space the parrots evenly along the dowelling, varying the lengths of ribbon to create a balanced effect. Suspend the mobile by tying a length of ribbon around the centre of the dowelling.

Toy Carrier

THIS STURDY BOX IS IDEAL FOR CARRYING AND STORING TOYS

YOU WILL NEED ■ *2 pieces of 22 × 16 cm (8¾ × 6¼ in) plywood, 10 mm (⅜ in) thick* ■ *Metal ruler* ■ *Pencil* ■ *Hand saw* ■ *Sandpaper* ■ *2 pieces of 35 × 12 cm (13½ × 4¾ in) plywood, 10 mm (⅜ in) thick* ■ *33.5 × 14.5 cm (13 × 5¾ in) plywood, 10 mm (⅜ in) thick* ■ *Wood glue* ■ *2.5 cm (1 in) panel pins (finishing nails)* ■ *Hammer* ■ *13.5 × 2.5 cm (5¼ × 1 in) square softwood batten* ■ *Hand drill* ■ *2 × 4.5 cm (1¾ in) screws* ■ *Plastic wood* ■ *Matt white emulsion (flat latex) paint* ■ *Paintbrushes* ■ *Non-toxic enamel paints*

2 Smooth down the softwood handle piece with sandpaper and position at the top of the end pieces. Drill in each end to accept the screws. Fix together using glue and screws, countersinking and filling the heads with plastic wood.

1 Take the 22 × 16 cm (8¾ × 6¼ in) pieces (the box ends) and make marks at 7 cm (2¾ in) and 9 cm (3½ in) on 1 shorter side. Mark 12.5 cm (5 in) on both longer sides. Rule diagonals to join the marks and saw off the triangles. Sand the tops into smooth corners. Join together an end piece, a 35 × 12 cm (13½ × 4¾ in) side piece and the base piece using wood glue and panel pins (finishing nails). Note that the sides and ends overlap the base. Repeat the same process with the other side and end.

3 Give the carrier a final sanding and paint on a coat of matt white emulsion (flat latex) paint. Allow to dry then finish with 2 coats of enamel paint in bright colours. Use a light colour for the inside so that small toys can be seen more easily.

SIDE PIECE - CUT 2

END PIECE
CUT 2

BASE - CUT 1

Peg Dolls

MAKE WASHDAY MORE FUN WITH THESE SIMPLE DECORATED PEG DOLLS

YOU WILL NEED ■ *Sandpaper* ■ *Old-fashioned clothes pegs (pins)* ■ *Matt emulsion (flat latex)*
paint ■ *Paintbrushes* ■ *Non-toxic acrylic paints* ■ *Non-toxic clear acrylic varnish*

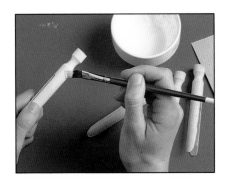

1 Sand down each peg (pin) with sandpaper to smooth any rough edges. Using the white emulsion (flat latex) paint, coat the pegs (pins) evenly.

2 With acrylic paint and a fine brush, paint on the doll's features and clothes: paint the face on the top round piece and the body and legs further down with the shoes at the bottom. Leave to dry thoroughly.

3 Lastly, paint on a protective coat of clear acrylic varnish. Hang all the completed pegs (pins) on the line and have fun hanging out the washing!

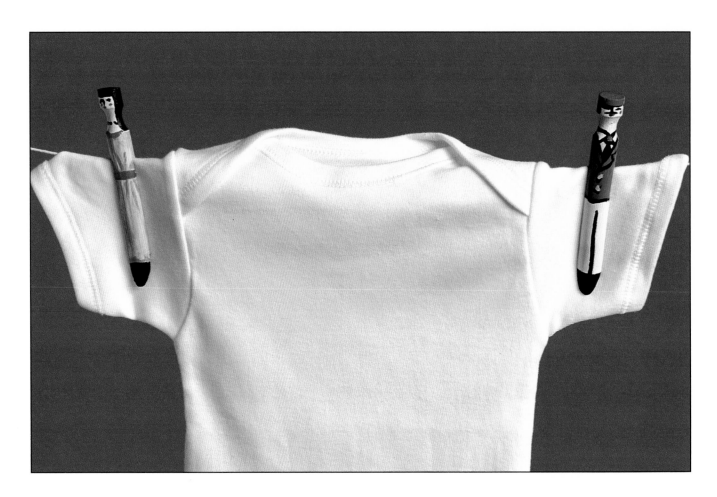

26 FUN IDEAS FOR EVERYDAY

Cat Blackboard

THE ATTRACTIVE SHAPE OF THIS BLACKBOARD WILL ENCOURAGE CHILDREN TO DRAW

YOU WILL NEED ■ *Pencil* ■ *Paper* ■ *Scissors* ■ *20 × 42 cm (8 × 16½ in) plywood,*
1.5 cm (⅝ in) thick ■ *Sticky putty* ■ *Fretsaw (scroll saw)* ■ *Sandpaper* ■ *Matt white emulsion (flat
latex) paint* ■ *Paintbrushes* ■ *Blackboard paint* ■ *Non-toxic white acrylic paint* ■ *Chalk*

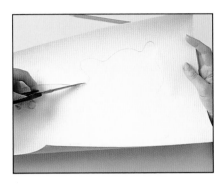

1 Draw a cat shape onto a sheet of paper and cut it out.

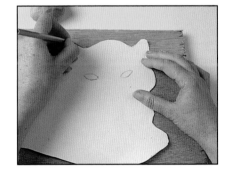

3 Cut out the cat shape with a fretsaw (scroll saw) and sand the edges with sandpaper to give a smooth finish.

2 Attach the template to the plywood with sticky putty and draw around it in pencil.

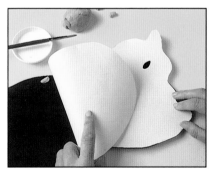

4 Using white emulsion (flat latex) and then 2 coats of blackboard paint, paint one side and all around the edges. Allow to dry between coats. Mark the eyes on the template and cut them out. Lay the template over the cut shape and paint in the outline of the eyes with white acrylic paint. Lastly paint the whiskers with a fine brush. Supply sticks of chalk for drawing on the board.

Kite Box

KEEP THE NURSERY TIDY WITH THIS ATTRACTIVE STORAGE BOX

YOU WILL NEED ■ *Hat box* ■ *Large paintbrush* ■ *Matt emulsion (flat latex) paint*
■ *Yellow paper* ■ *Non-toxic acrylic paints* ■ *Small paintbrush* ■ *Pencil* ■ *Ruler* ■ *Scissors*
■ *Paper glue* ■ *Natural sponge* ■ *Non-toxic clear acrylic varnish*

1 Paint the box with the matt emulsion (flat latex) paint and, while this is drying, paint some yellow paper with red paint allowing streaks of background colour to come through giving an orange glow.

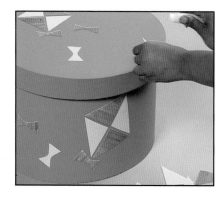

2 Using the templates as a guide, draw equal numbers of triangular and ribbon shapes onto the orange paper and the yellow paper. Cut out all the shapes and glue onto the box to make the kite pattern.

3 Using white paint, carefully sponge on the cloud shapes with a natural sponge, making sure as you work that the sponge is not overloaded with paint.

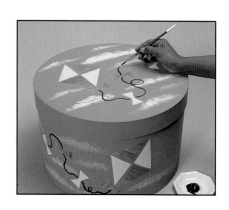

4 Paint in a fine dark line between the ribbons to make the kite string. Allow everything to dry, and finish with a protective coat of clear varnish.

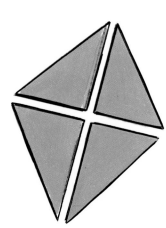

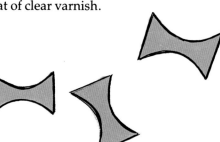

Ribbon Box

THE PERFECT BOX FOR ALL THOSE DISAPPEARING LITTLE SOCKS

YOU WILL NEED ■ *Hat box* ■ *Yellow matt emulsion (flat latex) paint* ■ *Paintbrushes* ■ *Chalk*
■ *Non-toxic acrylic paints* ■ *Non-toxic clear acrylic varnish*

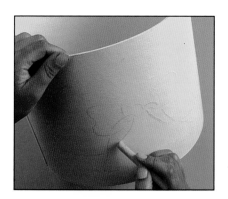

1 Paint the box with yellow matt emulsion (flat latex) and leave to dry. Chalk in the outline of the ribbon pattern.

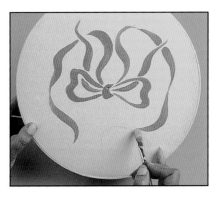

2 Using a small brush, follow the line of chalk with a dark coloured paint.

3 Allow to dry, then paint in the highlights of the ribbons with a lighter hue of the same colour. Leave to dry.

4 Finally, paint on a protective coat of clear acrylic varnish.

Hanging Shoe Tidy

AN ATTRACTIVE WAY TO KEEP TINY SHOES IN ORDER

YOU WILL NEED ■ *Tape measure* ■ *75 × 90 cm (30 × 36 in) fabric* ■ *Scissors*
■ *Pins* ■ *Needle and thread* ■ *75 cm (30 in) elastic* ■ *Safety pins* ■ *43 × 65 cm (17 × 26 in) stiff card*
■ *Rubber-based glue* ■ *Hole punch* ■ *45 cm (18 in) ribbon, 2.5 cm (1 in) wide*

2 Run a line of gathering stitches along the bottom edge of each pocket strip. Adjust the gathering until each strip measures 43 cm (17 in).

3 With right sides together, sew a strip 2.5 cm (1 in) from the bottom of the back piece. Pull the strip up, fold down the edges and sew to the back piece with 15 mm (5/8 in) side seams. Sew the 6 marked positions to form the pockets. Make the second pocket in the same way.

Cut the top 25 cm (10 in) of the cardboard into a triangle and spread with glue. Stretch the back piece of fabric over the cardboard and allow to dry. Trim the fabric corners, then spread glue around the board edges and glue down the edges of the fabric. Punch a hole 5 cm (2 in) from the top and thread a ribbon through.

1 Cut the fabric into 2 strips for the pockets, 18 × 75 cm (7 × 30 in) and 1 main piece, 45 × 65 cm (18 × 26 in), cutting the top 20 cm (8 in) of the main piece into a triangle. Sew a 2.5 cm (1 in) hem along the top of both pocket strips.

Mark the 6 positions for the pocket seams with pins so that you will end up with 8 pockets. Cut the elastic in half and thread a length through each hem, securing it 15 mm (5/8 in) short of the sides with a safety pin.

Balloons Toy Bag

A USEFUL BAG TO KEEP SMALL TOYS TIDY

YOU WILL NEED ■ *Pinking shears* ■ *50 × 90 cm (½ yd × 36 in) striped cotton fabric* ■ *Iron-on double-sided interfacing* ■ *Oddments of 3 plain coloured fabrics* ■ *Iron* ■ *Pair of compasses* ■ *Pencil* ■ *Scissors* ■ *Needle and thread* ■ *Pins* ■ *40 cm (16 in) each of ribbon in 3 colours, 3 mm (⅛ in) wide* ■ *2 m (80 in) of ribbon, 1.5 cm (⅝ in) wide* ■ *Safety pin*

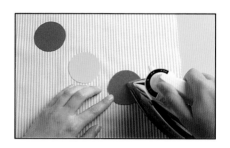

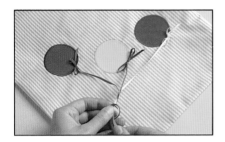

1 Cut out two 43 × 34 cm (17 × 13½ in) rectangles of striped fabric with pinking shears. Apply iron-on interfacing to each oddment of plain fabric following the manufacturer's instructions. Use a pair of compasses to draw 6 cm (2½ in) circles on the backing paper. Cut out the 3 balloons.

Peel off the backing paper and arrange the balloons centrally on the right side of 1 of the striped rectangles. Press the balloons to bond them in position. Stitch the balloons to the bag around the circumference.

2 With right sides facing, stitch the rectangles together leaving the upper short edge open and a 2 cm (¾ in) gap 3 cm (1¼ in) below the upper edge on the long sides. Press the seams open. Fold down the upper edge to the wrong side by 3 cm (1¼ in) and pin in place to make a channel for the drawstring. Stitch the channel 2 cm (¾ in) below the folded edge.

3 Turn the bag right side out. Tie one end of each of the narrow ribbons into a bow. Sew each bow to a balloon. Arrange the ribbons on the bag and knot the extending ends together. Sew the knot to the bag. Cut off the surplus ribbon.

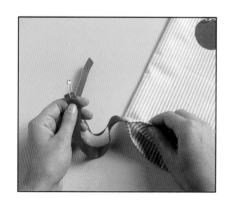

4 Cut the length of wide ribbon in half. Fix a safety pin to the end of one ribbon and thread through an opening in the channel, take all around the channel and bring the pin out through the same hole. Knot the ribbon ends together. Thread the remaining ribbon through the other hole in the same way; knot the ribbon ends together. Pull the ribbons to hide the knots in the channel.

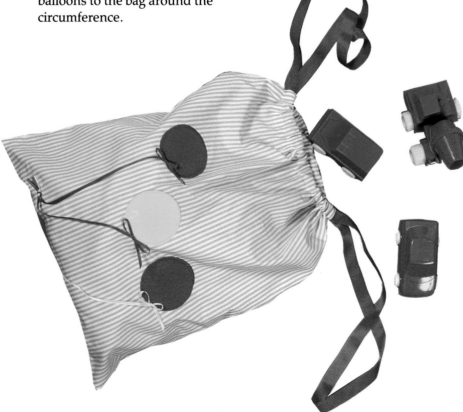

Nightclothes Case

A HAPPY BRIGHT CAT TO CUDDLE AND KEEP NIGHTCLOTHES NEAT AND TIDY

YOU WILL NEED ■ *Pen* ■ *Paper* ■ *Tape measure* ■ *Scissors* ■ *Cotton fabrics in bright reds and blues* ■ *Pins* ■ *Needle and thread* ■ *Iron* ■ *Zip (zipper)* ■ *Gingham fabric* ■ *Wadding (batting)* ■ *Oddments of felt* ■ *Embroidery thread*

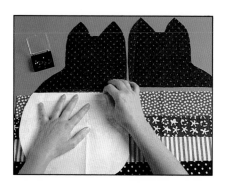

1 The size of this bag can be adjusted as you wish so that larger nightclothes can fit inside. The smallest reasonable size is about 45 cm (18 in) tall. Make a paper pattern of the required size for the cat shape, using the template as a guide, and work out the length and width you will need for the patchwork strips,

remembering to add seam allowances of about 1 cm (⅜ in). The strips must be long enough to make both sides of the cat. With the right sides together, join the strips accurately and then press the seams so that they lie flat. Cut 2 opposite cat head shapes and use your pattern to cut 2 opposite bodies from the patchwork strips.

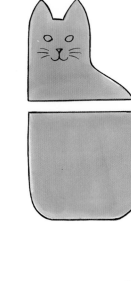

2 With right sides together, join the heads to the bodies and press the seams open. With right sides together, pin the straight edges of the cat together and make a 2 cm (¾ in) long seam at the top (from where the curve of the ear becomes straight) and the same on the straight at the bottom of the seam. Tack (baste) and sew them using a 1 cm (⅜ in) seam allowance. Press back seam allowances of 1 cm (⅜ in) all the way up the fronts which prepares

the opening for the zip (zipper). Position the closed zip (zipper) centrally with the cat body opened up flat, and tack (baste) it into place. Stitch the zip (zipper) from the right side. Fold the cat along the zip (zipper) with right sides together and pin, tack (baste) and sew the body together. Turn it to the right side through the open zip (zipper) and press the outside seam flat, picking out the points at the ears if necessary with a pin to make them sharp.

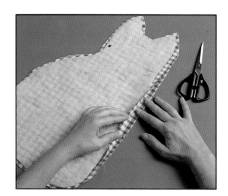

3 Cut 2 complete opposite body shapes from gingham for the bag lining. Cut a piece of wadding (batting) the same size and then trim it down about 1 cm ($^3/_8$ in) all the way round. Pin, tack (baste) and sew the lining with right sides together, leaving an opening unstitched. Do not turn to the right side.

Place the wadding (batting) on top. Insert the lining into the cat's body, tucking the wadding (batting) up into the ears and smoothing it flat inside. Remove and re-trim if necessary.

4 Turn the lining opening under and tack (baste) it down round the opening, ensuring that the zip (zipper) runs freely. Cut felt for the eyes and nose and sew them to the head through to the lining which will help keep it in place. Embroider a mouth and whiskers. Backstitches or a few French knots can also be worked on the patchwork strips through to the lining.

Flower Pot Tidy

STORE SMALL TOYS IN THESE HANDY FLOWER POT POCKETS

YOU WILL NEED ■ *Scissors* ■ *45 × 90 cm (½ yd × 36 in) contrasting fabric* ■ *Tape measure*
■ *Pins* ■ *Needle and thread* ■ *60 cm (24 in) ric-rac braid* ■ *2 pieces 45 × 90 cm (½ yd × 36 in) fabric*
■ *Oddments of brightly coloured felt* ■ *Embroidery thread* ■ *36 cm (14 in) ribbon or fabric binding*

1 Use the template to cut out 8 flower pot shapes from the contrasting fabric. Each pot should be 21 cm (8½ in) high and 12 cm (4¾ in) wide at the top. Sew in pairs, leaving a gap at the top for turning right side out.

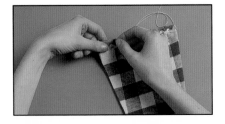

2 Cut the ric-rac braid into 4, and sew a length along the top edge of each flower pot.

3 Sew the flower pots onto one of the large pieces of background fabric. Cut flower shapes from the oddments of felt, using the templates as a guide. Pin the shapes into position and then sew on using embroidery thread in contrasting colours.

4 Cut 3 loops from the ribbon or fabric binding. Pin both sides of the background pieces right sides together, and sandwich the ends of the 3 loops along the top edge. Sew the 2 pieces together leaving a gap and then turn right side out. Sew up the gap.

Scented Mobile

THESE PRETTY BUTTERFLIES ARE BOTH DECORATIVE AND PRACTICAL

YOU WILL NEED ■ *Pencil* ■ *Paper* ■ *Pinking shears* ■ *Wadding (batting)* ■ *Scraps of plain and patterned fabrics* ■ *Pins* ■ *Needle and thread* ■ *Pot pourri* ■ *Dowelling (optional)*

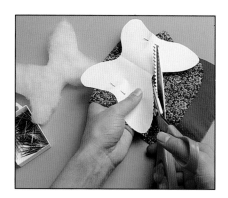

1 Scale up the template and transfer onto paper. Use this to cut out several butterflies from wadding (batting). Place a piece of patterned fabric onto plain fabric and pin on the pattern. Cut out the butterfly shape using pinking shears. Repeat with different combinations of fabric.

2 Sandwich the wadding (batting) between each pair of fabric butterfly pieces, pin in position and tack (baste) around the edge, taking a 6 mm ($\frac{1}{4}$ in) seam allowance and leaving a 5 cm (2 in) gap in the upper wing. Spoon the pot pourri into the gap and shake well.

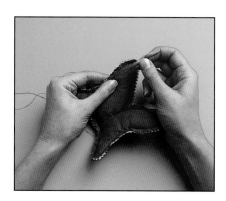

3 Top stitch neatly around the edge of each butterfly, taking a 6 mm ($\frac{1}{4}$ in) seam. Fold each butterfly in half, and then use a double thread to stitch through the centre of each as shown, to keep the folded shape. Attach a single thread to each wing 2.5 cm (1 in) from the tip and knot securely. Hang the butterflies directly from the ceiling or from a piece of wooden dowelling.

Geese Photo Frame

THIS CHARMING FRAME WILL ENHANCE ANY BABY'S PHOTOGRAPH

YOU WILL NEED ■ *Craft knife* ■ *Pencil* ■ *Mounting board* ■ *Ruler*
■ *Brown parcel tape* ■ *Newspaper, torn into short strips* ■ *Thin wallpaper paste*
■ *Thin card* ■ *Rubber-based glue* ■ *Acrylic gesso* ■ *Non-toxic acrylic paints* ■ *Paintbrushes*
■ *Natural sponge* ■ *Non-toxic clear acrylic varnish*

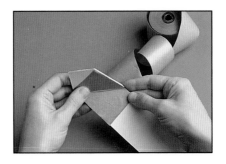

1 Use a craft knife to cut out the frame from mounting board, using the templates as a guide. Make a hinge on the stand using brown parcel tape.

2 Make a ridge of newspaper on the back piece, 4 cm (1½ in) from the edge (this will support the photograph). Cover all the pieces with two layers of newspaper strips dipped in thin wallpaper paste. Assemble the frame pieces with strips of pasted newspaper and allow to dry overnight away from direct heat. Glue the frame stand to the back piece and strengthen it with more papier mâché.

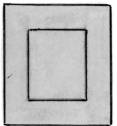
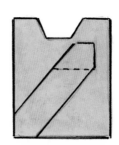

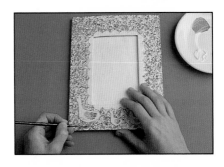

3 Cut the border and geese from thin card, glue in place and cover with a layer of papier mâché. Allow to dry and paint with acrylic gesso.

4 Apply green and yellow paint to the frame using a sponge. Paint the white border and the geese, and allow to dry. Finish with 2 coats of varnish.

Apple Tree Hooks

THESE CHARMING COAT HOOKS ENCOURAGE TODDLERS TO BE TIDY

YOU WILL NEED ■ *Pencil* ■ *Paper* ■ *Scissors* ■ *Plyboard, 6 mm (¼ in) thick*
■ *Sticky putty* ■ *Fretsaw (scroll saw)* ■ *Sandpaper* ■ *Matt white emulsion (flat latex) paint*
■ *Paintbrush* ■ *Non-toxic acrylic paints* ■ *3 red wooden doorknobs (or red-painted plain doorknobs)*
■ *Hand drill* ■ *Non-toxic acrylic varnish* ■ *Picture hook*

3 Once the primer is dry, paint the top of the tree green and the trunk an ochre colour. Leave to dry.

1 Draw the shape of a tree onto the paper, using the template as a guide. Cut it out and stick it on to the plyboard with sticky putty. Draw around the template with a pencil.

4 Mark in the positions for the 3 doorknobs and drill a small hole for each with the hand drill. Screw in the knobs from the back and varnish with a coat of non-toxic varnish. Attach to the wall using a picture hook.

2 Cut out the shape with a fretsaw (scroll saw) and rub down the edges with sandpaper wrapped around a block of wood. Prime with a coat of matt white emulsion (flat latex) paint.

Cat Book-ends

THE PURRFECT WAY TO ORGANIZE FAVOURITE STORY BOOKS

YOU WILL NEED ■ *Tracing paper* ■ *Pencil* ■ *Thin plywood*
■ *Ruler* ■ *Fretsaw (scroll saw)* ■ *Sandpaper* ■ *Wood glue* ■ *Hammer* ■ *Small tacks* ■ *Non-toxic acrylic paint* ■ *Paintbrushes* ■ *Non-toxic clear acrylic varnish*

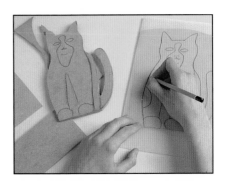  

1 Scale up the cat design from the template onto tracing paper. Trace 2 cat shapes onto the plywood and mark an extra rectangular piece 10×26 cm ($4 \times 10\frac{1}{4}$ in). Cut out the 3 shapes using a fretsaw (scroll saw) and sand down any rough edges.

2 Spread wood glue onto both ends of the rectangular piece of wood, then using a hammer and three small tacks for each end, nail the cat ends securely to the rectangular base. Allow to dry for at least 2 hours.

3 Paint the whole piece black and allow to dry before adding the cat's features in different colours. Finally, paint on a protective coat of clear acrylic varnish and leave to dry.

Bright Hangers

HAVE FUN HANGING UP YOUR BABY'S CLOTHES!

YOU WILL NEED ■ *Small paintbrush* ■ *Non-toxic acrylic paints* ■ *2 plain wooden coathangers*
■ *Plastic gems and sequins* ■ *Rubber-based glue*

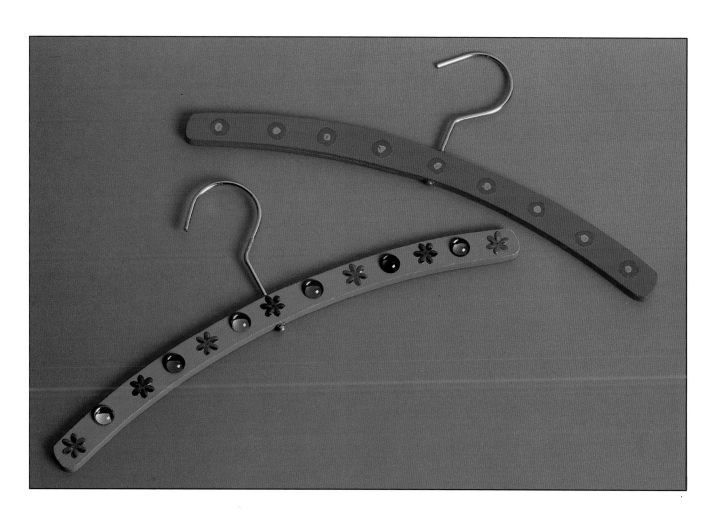

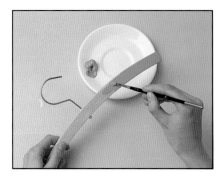

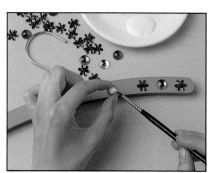

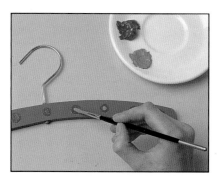

1 For the gem and sequin hanger, first paint your chosen colour onto the hanger and allow it to dry.

2 Stick on the gems and sequins alternately using rubber-based glue applied with a small brush, and allow to dry.

3 For the painted hanger, simply paint on a background coat of paint and allow it to dry. Finish by painting on a pattern of dots in 2 bright contrasting colours.

Circus Toiletries Bag

THIS JOLLY CLOWN MOTIF WILL LIVEN UP BATHTIME

YOU WILL NEED ■ *50.5 × 16 cm (20 × 6¼ in) piece of plasticized fabric*
■ *Tape measure* ■ *Rubber-based glue* ■ *Clothes pegs (pins)* ■ *Scissors* ■ *Oddments of plasticized*
fabric in red, green, yellow, blue, black and pale yellow or white ■ *Pencil* ■ *Velcro*

1 Fold the large piece of fabric in half widthways, leaving an 8 cm (3¼ in) overlap. Fold each corner of the overlap over and glue. Use clothes pegs (pins) to hold them while they dry.

3 Cut out an 8 cm (3¼ in) red circle and glue it to the front of the bag, placing it 4 cm (1½ in) from the bottom. Cut out the shapes for the clown's hat, face and features and glue them in place over the red circle.

4 To make the fastening, glue small strips of Velcro to the underside of the red circle and the front of the bag.

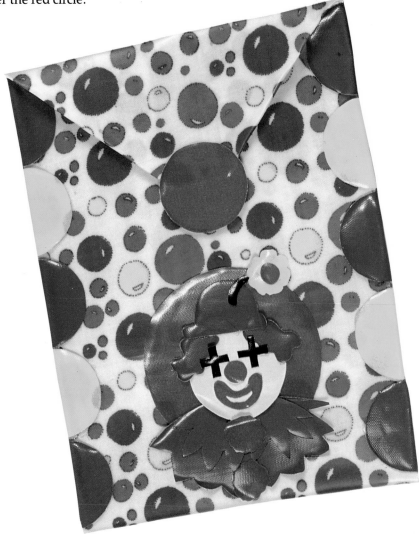

2 Cut out 2 blue circles, 4 green circles, 4 yellow circles, all 4 cm (1½ in) in diameter. Spread glue onto the back of each one and start by placing half of one green circle under the back of the bag. Fold the other half over to the front and press. Secure with a peg (pin).

Continue with the yellow circle, then blue, then the green and yellow again. Repeat on the other side. Remove pegs (pins) when dry. Cut out 2 red circles 4 cm (1½ in) in diameter. Glue them together, encasing the point of the flap between the two.

High Chair Mat

THIS PRACTICAL MAT WILL SAVE THE FLOOR FROM UNWANTED SPILLS

YOU WILL NEED ■ *Pinking shears* ■ *100 × 75 cm (40 × 30 in) fabric* ■ *100 × 75 cm (40 × 30 in) coloured PVC (vinyl-coated) fabric* ■ *100 × 75 cm (40 × 30 in) clear PVC (vinyl) plastic* ■ *Scissors* ■ *Oddments of fabric and felt* ■ *Rubber-based glue* ■ *Needle and thread*

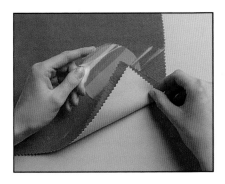

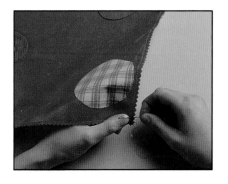

1 Cut out all the fabric pieces, cutting the larger pieces out with pinking shears. Cut fabric for as many spots as you like. Glue the small felt spots onto the larger spots and glue the spots onto the large piece of fabric.

2 Sandwich this fabric between a piece of coloured PVC (vinyl-coated) fabric and clear PVC (vinyl) plastic.

3 Sew all around the edges to attach all 3 layers, either by hand or using a machine set on a fairly loose tension.

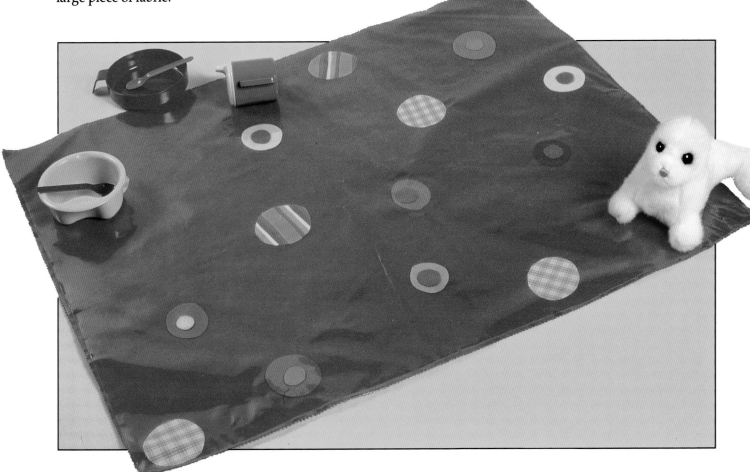

Beaker Mat

THIS WIPE-CLEAN MAT CAN BE USED ON A HIGH CHAIR

YOU WILL NEED ■ *Pencil* ■ *Scissors* ■ *Paper* ■ *Ruler* ■ *Pinking shears* ■ *10 × 10 cm (4 × 4 in)*
felt ■ *Clear PVC (vinyl) plastic* ■ *Oddments of felt* ■ *Rubber-based glue* ■ *Needle and thread*

1 Using the template as a guide, draw and cut out a starfish shape from white paper. Draw around the templates onto the materials and cut out 1 square in felt and 2 in PVC (vinyl) plastic using pinking shears, and cut 1 starfish in felt using scissors. Cut out some felt spots.

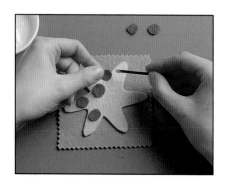

2 Glue the starfish onto the felt mat and then glue the felt spots onto its body. Press the spots down firmly to secure, as these small shapes can fall off during use if they are not well attached at the start.

3 Trap the felt in between the 2 pieces of clear PVC (vinyl) plastic and sew around the edge.

Place Mat

THIS PRACTICAL MAT WILL MAKE MEALTIMES SIMPLE

YOU WILL NEED ■ *Pencil* ■ *Paper* ■ *Scissors* ■ *Oddments of felt*
■ *Rubber-based glue* ■ *Large sequin* ■ *26 × 20 cm (10¼ × 8 in) felt* ■ *2 pieces of 26 × 20 cm*
(10¼ × 8 in) clear PVC (vinyl) plastic ■ *Pinking shears* ■ *Needle and thread*

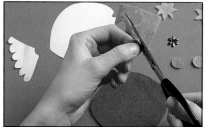

1 Using the templates as a guide, cut out the fish shapes in felt, and then cut out the spots and stars in contrasting colours. Assemble the fish using rubber-based glue, and add the large sequin for the eye.

2 Cut out the mat pieces using pinking shears and glue the fish and stars onto the felt piece.

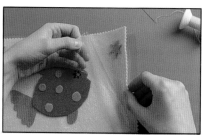

3 Trap the felt between 2 pieces of clear PVC (vinyl) plastic and sew around the edge through all 3 layers.

Egg Cosies

KEEP THE BREAKFAST EGGS HOT WITH THESE FUN EGG COSIES

YOU WILL NEED ■ *Scissors* ■ *Plain paper* ■ *Marker pen*
■ *Assorted pieces of coloured felt* ■ *Contrasting coloured felt for the hearts, spots and spikes*
■ *Needle and embroidery thread* ■ *3 flower-shaped sequins* ■ *Thread*

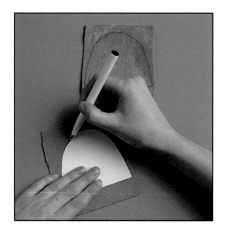  

1 Cut out an egg cosy shape from plain paper. Use it as a template and cut 2 shapes from the felt for each cosy.

2 Cut out the hearts, spots and spikes, and then sew the felt spots and sequins neatly onto one of the felt shapes using embroidery thread.

3 Fasten the cut-out hearts onto the other piece with small stitches.

4 Position one edge of each felt spike in between the two sides of the egg cosy and sew the 3 layers together. Turn inside out. If the cosy should become dirty in use, it can be washed in lukewarm water and allowed to dry naturally, but this should be done as infrequently as possible.

Plastic Bib

A FUN, WIPE-CLEAN BIB FOR MEALTIMES

YOU WILL NEED ■ Paper ■ Pen ■ Scissors ■ 20 × 24 cm
(8 × 9½ in) fabric ■ 20 × 24 cm (8 × 9½ in) coloured plastic fabric ■ 20 × 24 cm
(8 × 9½ in) clear PVC (vinyl) plastic ■ Oddments of felt ■ Rubber-based glue ■ Needle and thread
■ 2 metal eyelets ■ Hammer ■ 50 cm (19½ in) cord

1 Cut out a bib shape in paper. Draw around the pattern on the different fabrics and cut out 1 fabric and 2 plastic bib pieces. Cut a heart and some spots out of felt.

2 Glue the heart onto the fabric and glue the spots onto the heart.

3 Trap the fabric between the coloured and clear plastic and sew around the edges.

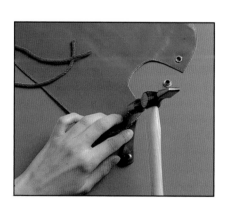

4 Attach 2 metal eyelets to the top edges of the bib with a hammer on a hard surface. Thread a piece of cord through each hole and tie a knot to each end of the cord to secure.

Bear **C**rayon **H**older

A DECORATIVE LITTLE HOLDER FOR CRAYONS OR PENS

YOU WILL NEED ■ *Scissors* ■ *Brown, orange, red and yellow gummed paper* ■ *Cardboard tube from a toilet paper roll* ■ *Soft cloth* ■ *White card* ■ *Pencil* ■ *Black felt-tip pen*

2 Cut out 2 oval shapes for the feet and a bear's head from the card. Place the card onto orange and brown gummed paper and draw around the card shape with a pencil. Cut out the gummed paper and stick it on to the relevant card shapes, using orange for the bear's feet and brown for the head.

1 Cut a piece of brown gummed paper to fit exactly around the cardboard tube, allowing for a small overlap at the join. Stick the paper down onto the tube using a damp cloth to moisten the gummed side.

3 Add an orange belly and a red nose and mouth plus two yellow eyes, all cut out from gummed paper and stuck to the card as before by moistening the gum with a damp cloth. Glue the feet to the bottom edge and stick the head and belly onto the front of the body. Finally, draw on the eyes and claws with black felt-tip pen. Leave the crayon holder to dry thoroughly before use.

Bean Bag Clown

THIS JOLLY CLOWN MAKES A HARDWEARING TOY

YOU WILL NEED ■ *Pencil* ■ *Paper* ■ *Scissors* ■ *20 × 90 cm (8 × 36 in) printed fabric* ■ *Scraps of coloured and white fabric* ■ *Paintbrush* ■ *Fabric paints* ■ *Iron* ■ *Needle and thread* ■ *Polystyrene (styrofoam) ball-bearings or dried peas* ■ *Oddments of felt* ■ *Pinking shears* ■ *Embroidery thread*

1 Scale up the templates onto paper and use as patterns. Cut 2 bodies from printed fabric, 2 hats from coloured fabric and 2 heads from white fabric. Lightly pencil the facial features onto 1 head piece and paint with fabric paints. Leave to dry then press the design carefully, following the manufacturer's instructions.

2 With right sides together, stitch each head to a hat and body, stitching between the dots on the template and leaving a 6 mm (¼ in) seam allowance. Press the seams towards the hat. With right sides together, stitch the clowns together leaving a 6 mm (¼ in) seam allowance and also leaving a 4 cm (1¾ in) gap to turn on one outside leg. Stitch again to reinforce the seam and trim.

3 Turn the clown right side out and fill with polystyrene (styrofoam) ball-bearings or dried peas. Sew up the gap to close.

4 Cut two 2 cm (¾ in) diameter circles from felt using pinking shears. Using embroidery thread, sew each circle to the front of the clown with a cross stitch, for the buttons.

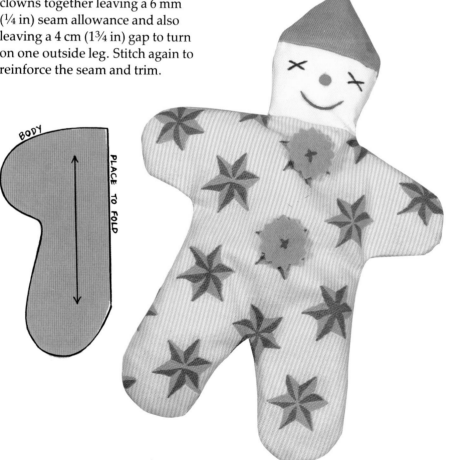

Alphabet **B**ricks

A FUN WAY TO LEARN THE ALPHABET FOR 1 TO 3-YEAR-OLDS

YOU WILL NEED ■ *5 × 5 cm (2 × 2 in) pine cut into squares* ■ *Sandpaper* ■ *Chalk* ■ *Small paintbrush* ■ *Non-toxic brightly coloured acrylic paints* ■ *Non-toxic clear acrylic varnish*

1 Take your squares of wood and use sandpaper to smooth down any rough edges.

2 Lightly chalk on the outlines of the letters and fill in the colours with a small brush. If you feel confident enough, just paint straight onto the squares.

3 Varnish the bricks with a protective coat of clear acrylic varnish and leave to dry.

Snake Glove Puppet

CREATE HOURS OF FUN FOR 2 TO 3-YEAR-OLDS WITH THIS ENTERTAINING PUPPET

YOU WILL NEED ■ *Squares of green, brown, red, black and yellow felt* ■ *Chalk*
■ *Scissors* ■ *Needle and embroidery thread* ■ *Pins* ■ *Rubber-based glue*

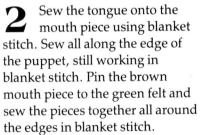

2 Sew the tongue onto the mouth piece using blanket stitch. Sew all along the edge of the puppet, still working in blanket stitch. Pin the brown mouth piece to the green felt and sew the pieces together all around the edges in blanket stitch.

1 Fold the green felt square in half and draw out the shape of the snake in chalk. Cut out the 2 pieces. Fold the brown felt and draw around the top of the green shape on the folded edge to make the inside of the mouth. Cut this shape out. Draw out the shapes of the tongue and the eyes as well as the 'V'-shapes for the back of the snake with a piece of coloured chalk on the red, black and yellow felt and cut out.

3 Finally, glue the eyes and the 'V'-shapes onto the back of the glove puppet.

Jacob's Ladder

THIS TOY WILL FASCINATE CHILDREN AND ADULTS ALIKE

*YOU WILL NEED ■ Fretsaw (scroll saw) ■ 42 × 4.5 cm (16½ × 1¾ in) wood,
1 cm (⅜ in) thick ■ Ruler ■ Fine sandpaper ■ Scissors ■ 140 cm (55 in) red ribbon, 6 mm (¼ in) wide
■ 70 cm (28 in) green ribbon, 6 mm (¼ in) wide ■ Rubber-based glue*

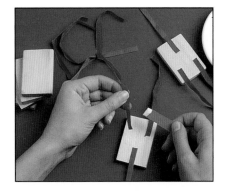

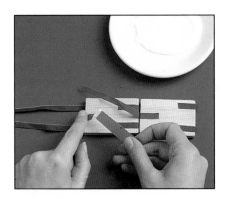

1 Cut the piece of wood into 6 equal sections, each measuring 7 cm (2¾ in) in length. Sand down all the edges until smooth with fine sandpaper, being careful of your hands on the rough surface.

2 Cut the red ribbon into 10 equal pieces, each 14 cm (5½ in) long. Cut the green ribbon into 5 equal pieces, each 14 cm (5½ in) long. Glue the ends of 2 pieces of red ribbon to one end of a piece of wood, 6 mm (¼ in) from the edges, and a length of green ribbon in the centre at the opposite end of the first section. Repeat with 4 more blocks.

3 Lay out all 6 pieces with alternate sides facing upwards. The piece with no ribbons goes at one end. Thread the ribbons under and over to connect all 6 pieces, gluing the ribbon tightly as you go.

Stacking Boxes

THIS EDUCATIONAL TOY IS SUITABLE FOR 2 TO 3-YEAR OLDS

YOU WILL NEED ■ *Wooden stacking boxes* ■ *Matt white emulsion*
(flat latex) paint ■ *Paintbrushes* ■ *Non-toxic acrylic paints in primary colours* ■ *Pencil* ■ *Card*
■ *Ruler* ■ *Scissors* ■ *Rubber-based glue* ■ *Non-toxic clear acrylic varnish*

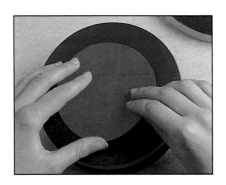

1 Paint the boxes with matt white emulsion (flat latex) paint to act as a base, leave to dry and then paint over the top in primary colours.

2 Draw out a different shape on the card for each box. Cut out each shape and paint in bright colours.

3 Glue the painted shapes onto the box lids. Make sure that the glue is completely dry, then varnish with a coat of clear acrylic varnish.

51

Elephant and Passenger

A CUDDLY ELEPHANT WITH A FUN SECRET PASSENGER

YOU WILL NEED ■ *Pen* ■ *Paper* ■ *Tape measure* ■ *Pins* ■ *Scissors*
■ *Polkadot cotton fabric* ■ *Washable satin fabric* ■ *Iron-on interfacing* ■ *Iron* ■ *Gingham*
■ *Needle and thread* ■ *Oddments of fabric for body and ears* ■ *Non-toxic, flame retardant polyester
filling (batting)* ■ *Length of plain cotton for the saddle strap* ■ *Cotton fabric for
the rider* ■ *Oddments of coloured felt* ■ *Embroidery thread* ■ *Ribbon*

1 Make paper patterns for all the required pieces, using the templates as a guide. Cut 2 opposite shapes in polkadot cotton for the bodies. Cut 2 opposite outer ears from the satin and use an iron-on interfacing on the reverse, being careful not to scorch the satin. Cut 2 opposite ear facings from the gingham.

Place the right sides together and stitch the 2 sets of ears, leaving the straight edges open. Turn them to the right side, press, and tack (baste) the openings closed. Check the position of the ears from the pattern and pin, tack (baste) and sew the ears in place on the opposite bodies.

2 Cut the gusset. With wrong sides together, fold the gusset in half matching the legs, and press. Pin, tack (baste) and stitch the gusset to the body and legs with right sides together, starting and finishing your stitch line at the opposite halfway marks folded into the gusset.

Cut 3 strips of cotton and satin fabrics each 12 cm (4¾ in) long and braid them together. Tie a knot just short of one end. Tack (baste) this tail to the body 9 cm (3½ in) above the gusset stitch line.

3 Place the second body on top of the first, right sides together, and tack (baste). To sew, open the gusset out flat to sew the second body side and stitch only the gusset section as before. Break off, fold the gusset back in half, then sew around the upper body, trunk and head. Leave a gap of 10 cm (4 in) for turning. Clip the curves and turn the body to the right side. Stuff firmly, and then oversew the opening.

4 Cut a piece of felt for the saddle about 14 × 10 cm (5½ × 4 in), and a flower shape with an inner circle in a different colour. Appliqué the decorations to the centre of one half of the saddle. Make a 4 cm (1½ in) wide saddle strap about 48 cm (19 in) long from the plain cotton. Sew the strap securely to the back of the saddle, so that you can conceal the overlapping ends behind the folded saddle. Fold the saddle wrong sides together and stitch the edges.

5 Make up the rider from 2 shapes sewn right sides together. Cut a small slit in the figure's back to turn, then stuff and oversew the opening. Embroider loops of hair onto the head and add eyes and mouth. Sew a felt sarong around the waist and a ribbon to the back. For safety, the ribbon should not be longer than about 12 cm (4¾ in). Sew the other end to the inside back of the saddle through to the strap so the rider can be hidden or brought out on the ribbon.

6 Arrange the saddle on the centre of the elephant, wind the strap around and then sew the strap ends together behind the saddle, carefully trimming away any excess to neaten. Hem the saddle to the body all the way round on both edges of the strap so that it cannot slip. Remember that children can be rough with their toys, so strong, secure stitching is essential. Finally, cut felt circles for the eyes and sew them to the head.

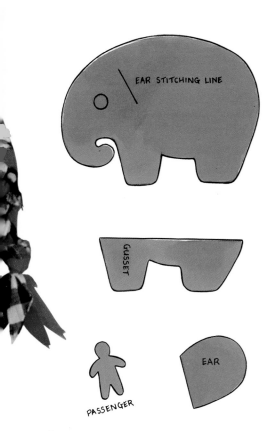

EAR STITCHING LINE

GUSSET

PASSENGER

EAR

Doing Doll

A CUDDLY DOLL WITH LOTS OF FASTENINGS

YOU WILL NEED ■ *Pen* ■ *Paper* ■ *Scissors* ■ *Pre-washed calico (cotton fabric)* ■ *Pins* ■ *Needle and thread* ■ *Non-toxic, flame retardant polyester filling (batting)* ■ *Tape measure* ■ *Card* ■ *Small quantity of yarn* ■ *Denim for the overalls* ■ *Iron* ■ *10 cm (4 in) zip (zipper) in a bright colour* ■ *Patterned cotton for patch, handkerchief and facings* ■ *Striped cotton for shirt and pocket* ■ *Pre-washed striped cotton for straps* ■ *Toggle* ■ *Large button* ■ *Scrap of fabric for toggle loop* ■ *Ribbon* ■ *Embroidery thread* ■ *Felt for eyes* ■ *Velcro*

1 Cut the paper patterns for all the pieces shown on the templates. Cut out 2 body shapes from calico (cotton fabric). Noting the position from the pattern, cut a slit in the body back. Pin, tack (baste) and stitch the body shapes right sides together. Clip the curves and turn the body right side out. Stuff firmly, pushing the filling well into the ends of the hands and feet.

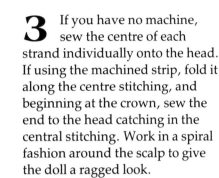

2 Cut a length of card 8 cm (3¼ in) wide and at least 20 cm (8 in) long. Wind the yarn around the whole length and cut through to form 16 cm (6¼ in) lengths. If you have a sewing machine, feed the yarn through the machine joining them together along the centre. You will need a length about 50 cm (19½ in) long.

3 If you have no machine, sew the centre of each strand individually onto the head. If using the machined strip, fold it along the centre stitching, and beginning at the crown, sew the end to the head catching in the central stitching. Work in a spiral fashion around the scalp to give the doll a ragged look.

4 Cut 2 opposites for each overalls shape, front and back, from the denim. Sew the first 3 cm (1¼ in) of the seam at the crotch of the overalls front. Press the seam flat and press the seam allowances back, making a crisp fold all the way up the front pieces of fabric.

Set the zip (zipper) behind the turned-back edges, pinning and tacking (basting) it neatly into place. Cut out a patch shape from patterned cotton and tack (baste) it to the left front. Cut a pocket flap and neaten it so that it measures about 6 × 3 cm (2¼ × 1¼ in). Cut and neaten a pocket to fit below the flap. Pin and tack (baste) the flap and pocket to the right front of the overalls.

5 Sew the zip (zipper), patch and pocket to the overalls. Make up the overalls back by joining the back seam. Trim the raw edges to 6 mm (¼ in) and oversew to neaten them. Turn the back waist edge down 1 cm (⅜ in), turn it under and stitch a hem.

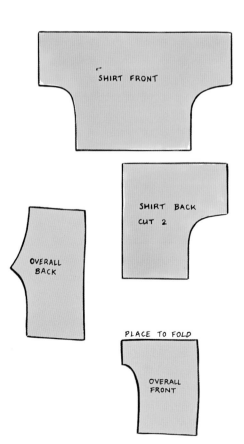

6 Matching leg hems and inner leg seams, pin and tack (baste) the side seams. The overalls front will be a little higher than the back at the waist. Stitch the side seams. Sew the inner leg seams. Trim all the raw edges to 6 mm (¼ in) and oversew to neaten them. Turn the overalls so that they are right side out.

Cut 2 opposite shapes from the selected fabric for the facings. Turn up a narrow hem. Matching the underarm curve and side seam, pin and tack (baste) the front facings to the overalls front, right sides together. The centre front edges will overlap the zip (zipper) opening by 1 cm (⅜ in). Stitch the top and underarm curves only, using a 1 cm (⅜ in) seam allowance. Clip the curves,

and then carefully trim the seam allowance to 6 mm (¼ in).

Turn the facings to the inside, turn them under at the side seams and zip (zipper) opening and hem them to the seam allowance. Make up 2 straps to cross over at the back. Sew on the toggle and button securely. Insert a small loop into the end of one strap to fasten the toggle and work a buttonhole in the other.

Cut out the shirt pieces, sew the side and shoulder seams and neaten all raw edges, leaving the back open. Sew ribbons to the top back. Embroider the doll's features, adding felt circles for the eyes. Make a handkerchief to put in the pocket and use Velcro on the pocket and flap so that it can be opened and closed.

Acrobatic Clown

THIS TRADITIONAL MOVING CLOWN MAKES A FASCINATING TOY

YOU WILL NEED ■ *Ruler* ■ *Pencil* ■ *Paper* ■ *Scissors* ■ *2 sheets of 20 × 15 cm (8 × 6 in)*
plywood, 6 mm (¼ in) thick ■ *Clamp* ■ *Hand drill* ■ *Fretsaw (scroll saw)* ■ *Length of dowelling, 5 mm (³⁄₁₆ in)*
in diameter ■ *Fine sandpaper* ■ *Non-toxic acrylic paints* ■ *Paintbrushes* ■ *Wood glue* ■ *Coloured string*

1 Scale up the clown templates onto paper and cut out. Draw around the body, leg and arm pieces onto one of the sheets of plywood. Clamp the 2 sheets together firmly, and then drill out the 4 × 5 mm (³⁄₁₆ in) holes in the body and 6 mm (¼ in) holes in the arms and legs. Cut and push two 2 cm (¾ in) lengths of dowelling into 2 of the body holes to help hold the sheets together before cutting out all the shapes.

2 Sand down the 2 arms, 2 legs and the bodies held together with dowelling with fine sandpaper. Remove the pieces of dowelling. Carefully paint the backs and fronts of the legs and arms, and paint a face on the front body and a back on the back body piece. Allow to dry.

3 Ensure that the holes in the arms and legs allow them to move freely on the dowelling and then drill a small hole in the top of each as indicated, and glue one end of a 20 cm (8 in) length of string in each.

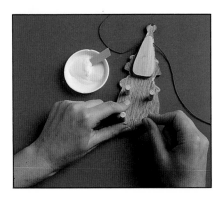

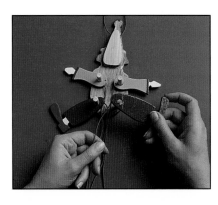

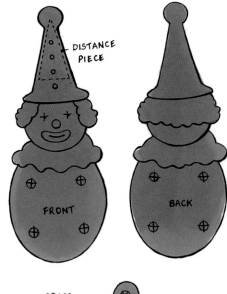

4 Place the front body piece face down. Cut out a triangular distance piece from the waste plywood, cross-drill a hole at the top and thread through the hanging string. Glue into position near the top of the 'hat'. Glue the 4 cut lengths of dowelling into the front body piece.

5 Attach the arms and legs onto the dowelling and draw all the strings down between the legs as shown. Put a little glue on the distance piece and in each of the holes in the back piece, and carefully press in position over the dowelling, making sure that the arms and legs move freely. When the glue has dried completely, smooth down the dowelling with a piece of sandpaper and cover the ends with a little paint.

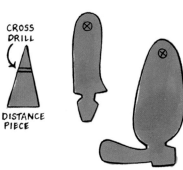

Shape Matcher

CHILDREN WILL ENJOY THE CHALLENGE OF MATCHING EACH SHAPE TO A POCKET

YOU WILL NEED ▪ *Scissors* ▪ *1 m (1 yd) white cotton fabric,*
115 cm (45 in) wide, washed and pressed ▪ *Ruler* ▪ *Needle and thread* ▪ *Pencil*
▪ *Card* ▪ *Red, yellow and blue fabric paints* ▪ *Natural sponge* ▪ *Iron* ▪ *0.5 m (½ yd)*
lightweight iron-on interfacing ▪ *Pins* ▪ *Wadding (batting)*

1 Cut out the pattern pieces from the fabric. Fold the 6 pocket pieces in half, with right sides together, and sew round 6 mm (¼ in) from the edge, leaving a small gap for turning. Trim the seams and clip the corners before turning out to the right side. Make the 6 ties in the same way and press all pieces.

2 Cut out 6 templates in card, drawing a different shape on each. Using a new colour for each shape, use the templates like stencils and print the pockets with a sponge and fabric paints. Print the shapes all over the main body piece and twice each on spare fabric for the soft shapes. Fix the dye by ironing.

3 Cut a piece of interfacing to the size of the printed main body and iron it on carefully, following the manufacturer's instructions. Pin the ties in position between the two main body pieces and sew all round. Turn through to the right way out and edge stitch. Position the pockets and stitch into place.

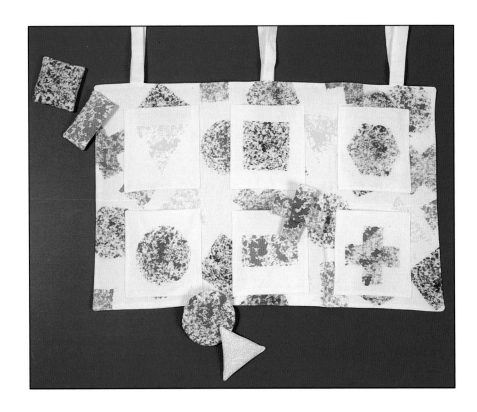

4 Cut out the printed shapes leaving a 6 mm (¼ in) seam (12 pieces). Pin them together in matching pairs, with right sides together, and tack (baste) wadding (batting) into place. Sew through all the layers, leaving a gap for turning. Trim all the edges and clip the corners. Turn through and oversew the gap securely.

Train Jigsaw

THIS EASILY MADE PUZZLE WILL PLEASE ANY 1 TO 3-YEAR-OLD

YOU WILL NEED ■ *Pencil* ■ *Paper* ■ *Ruler* ■ *Coloured card* ■ *Craft knife*
■ *Scissors* ■ *Coloured paper* ■ *Paper glue*

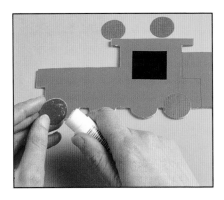

1 Scale up the train template onto paper to the required size and transfer this onto your coloured card. Cut out the whole shape of the train either with scissors or with a craft knife. Cut out square shapes for the windows and circles for the wheels and draw in the dividing lines between each carriage.

2 Glue down the shapes for the train's windows and wheels with paper glue.

3 Cut down the dividing lines using a craft knife and ruler to make the jigsaw pieces.

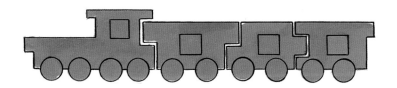

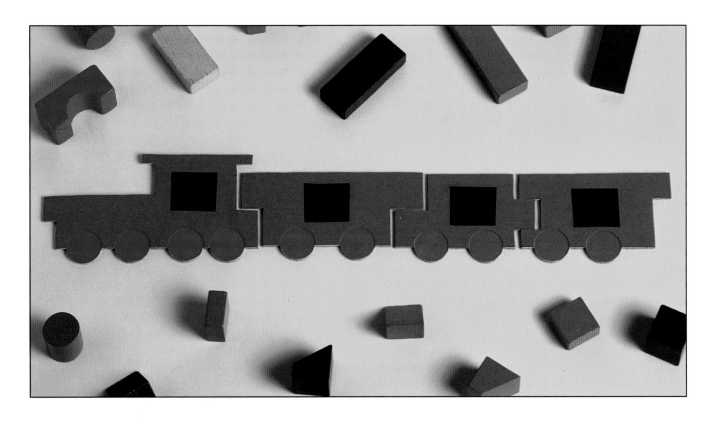

Rag Doll

THIS OLD-FASHIONED RAG DOLL IS SURE TO BECOME A TRUE FRIEND

YOU WILL NEED ■ *Pen* ■ *Paper* ■ *Tape measure* ■ *Scissors* ■ *Pre-washed calico (cotton fabric)* ■ *Pins* ■ *Needle and thread* ■ *Non-toxic, fire retardant polyester filling (batting)* ■ *Striped fabric for bloomers* ■ *Pretty cotton fabric for the dress* ■ *Contrasting fabric for patches* ■ *Elastic* ■ *Lace trimming* ■ *Card* ■ *Yarn* ■ *Ribbon* ■ *Oddments of felt* ■ *Embroidery thread* ■ *Velcro*

1 Cut out a paper pattern, using the template as a guide. Cut out 2 body shapes from the calico (cotton fabric). Cut a small slit in the body back. Pin, tack (baste) and stitch the body shapes together, clip the curves and turn the body right side out. Stuff the body firmly, pushing the filling well into the ends of the hands and feet.

VERTICAL SLIT

2 Cut out 2 pieces of striped fabric for the bloomers. Pin them right sides together and sew the curved seam with a 6 mm (¼ in) allowance. Oversew the raw edges. Cut a piece of fabric for the dress 85 × 26 cm (34 × 10¼ in) and several squares for patches.

Pin and appliqué these at random to the dress front. Make a back seam in the dress by joining the 2 shorter edges, leaving a small opening at the neck. Neaten the seam. Make 1 cm (⅜ in) hems at the top and bottom and mark the centre front with a pin.

3 Turn the bloomers so that the curved crotch seam is in the centre position with right sides together. Stitch and neaten the side seams. Make a narrow casing at the waist and insert a piece of elastic to fit round the doll's waist. Make a narrow casing at the leg bottoms and insert elastic to fit. Trim with lace.

4 Cut 2 lengths of card 4 cm (1½ in) and 10 cm (4 in) wide. Use the narrower width to make the fringe. Wind yarn around both cards and then cut through to form short lengths of yarn. Make enough for a fringe about 2.5 cm (1 in) long when the strands are laid side to side. You will need about 16 cm (6¼ in) for the hair. If you have a sewing machine, feed the fringe lengths through the machine, joining them together along the centre. Do the same with the hair lengths.

5 Put the doll in the dress with her arms out at the top. Catch the dress up at the sides from under the arms and make armholes by oversewing the back to the front at the shoulders. Gather the front and the back sections with a double thread to fit the doll, and stitch a line through the gathers to hold them securely.

6 If you have no machine, attach the hair by sewing each strand firmly in place. If using a machined strip, place it centrally down the back of the head with the stitching line as a 'parting'. Stitch, catching in the machined stitches as you go.

Fold the fringe strip along the centre stitching and sew it round the front of the head. Make 2 braids, secure and tie with 2 narrow ribbon bows. Sew the braids to the head. Cut felt for the eyes and cheeks and embroider the other features. Stitch a Velcro fastening to the sides of the dress back at the neck.

Cuddly Plane

AN UNUSUAL SOFT TOY THAT IS SUITABLE FOR A SMALL BABY

YOU WILL NEED ■ *Pen* ■ *Paper* ■ *Scissors* ■ *Pins* ■ *2 patterned cotton fabrics in contrasting colours* ■ *Wadding (batting)* ■ *Needle and thread* ■ *Iron* ■ *Non-toxic, flame retardant polyester filling (batting)* ■ *Oddments of black and white felt* ■ *Embroidery thread*

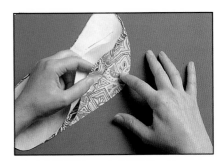

1 Make a paper pattern for the plane body, wings and tail fins using the template as a guide. Cut 2 opposite shapes for the body from 1 fabric and 4 each of the wing and fin shapes from the contrasting fabric. Cut 4 pieces of wadding (batting), 2 for the wings and 2 for the fins.

2 Place 2 wing shapes right sides together and lay a piece of wadding (batting) on the top. Stitch together, 6 mm (¼ in) from the edge, leaving the straight edge open. Make the second wing and 2 fins in the same way. Turn all shapes right side out and press carefully. Check the width of your wing and cut a slit in the plane body to exactly the same width, noting the position of the slit on the pattern. Fold the plane body along the slit with the right sides

together and insert the open wing end from the outside through to the inside of the slit. Pin and tack (baste). Start sewing from the folded edge about 4 mm (⅛ in) before the slit. Curve the seam out gently and sew through all layers so that at the centre of wing the stitches are about 4 mm (⅛ in) from the raw edge of the slit. Curve in again for the second half of the seam. Secure all threads firmly. Repeat this process for the second wing and the tail fins.

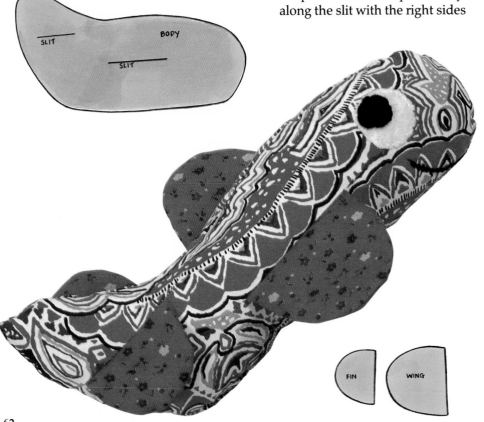

3 Place the plane bodies right sides together, and, tucking in the wings and fins, pin and tack (baste) them. Stitch the seam 1 cm (⅜ in) from the edge, leaving a short length on the underside for turning. Turn the body right side out. Stuff the plane firmly with filling and oversew the opening to close. Sew on felt circles for the eyes and embroider the mouth.

62

Shoe Lacer

A SIMPLE AID TO HELP CHILDREN LEARN TO TIE THEIR OWN SHOELACES

YOU WILL NEED ■ *Pencil* ■ *Tracing paper* ■ *10 × 20 cm (4 × 8 in) plywood, 8 mm ($^5/_{16}$ in) thick* ■ *Fretsaw (scroll saw)* ■ *Hand drill* ■ *Sandpaper* ■ *Matt white emulsion (flat latex) paint* ■ *Paintbrush* ■ *Non-toxic acrylic paints* ■ *58 cm (23 in) decorated shoelace*

  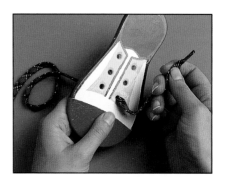

1 Scale up the shoe template and trace onto the plywood. Cut out carefully with the fretsaw (scroll saw). Place the shoe shape on a piece of scrap material and drill out the lace holes with a 6 mm (¼ in) bit. Sand out the top and bottom of the holes, and smooth the whole piece to get rid of any rough edges.

2 Paint the shoe shape all over with a coat of matt white emulsion (flat latex) paint. When dry, paint with 2 coats of different coloured acrylic paints, sanding lightly between each of the coats.

3 When the paint has dried completely, lace up the 'shoe' with a decorative, brightly coloured shoelace.

Noah's Ark Bag

A FUN NEW WAY TO TELL AN OLD STORY

YOU WILL NEED ■ *Assorted blue and white fabrics* ■ *Tape measure* ■ *Scissors* ■ *Pins* ■ *Needle and thread* ■ *Iron* ■ *Paper* ■ *Pencil* ■ *Iron-on interfacing* ■ *White felt* ■ *Green embroidery thread* ■ *Ribbon* ■ *Safety pin* ■ *Non-toxic, flame retardant polyester filling (batting)*

1 Choose 2 different fabrics for the bag front to represent sea and sky. Cut the sky 36 × 36 cm (14 × 14 in) and the sea 36 × 19 cm (14 × 7½ in). With right sides together, join the 2 fabrics along one long edge as shown. Press the seam to one side and oversew the raw edges together.

2 Cut paper templates for the design on the bag front. Cut out different fabric shapes for the ark using an iron-on interfacing on all the shapes to strengthen them. Cut the dove from white felt.

3 Assemble the cut shapes for the Ark on the bag front so that the boat appears to be floating on the sea. Pin them all in place, then tack (baste) and appliqué them to the bag. Sew the dove to the bag with tiny blanket stitches, and embroider the olive leaf with green thread.

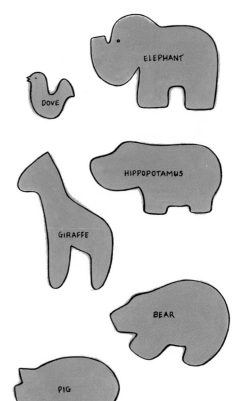

4 Cut a bag back to the same size as the assembled front. Stitch all round the bag back and front, right sides together, leaving the top edge open for turning. Trim the seam allowances and oversew the raw edges.

5 Turn the bag right side out. Fold down a casing at the top for the drawstring, wide enough to take your ribbon. Carefully unpick one side seam stitching inside where the casing turns over, to allow you to thread the ribbon through the drawstring using a safety pin at one end. Sew up the seam and tie the ends of the drawstring in a knot, neatening any ends. For reasons of safety, do not make the drawstring any longer than is necessary to open and shut the bag.

 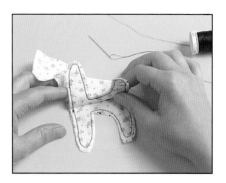 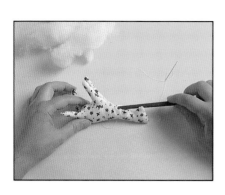

6 Make paper patterns for all the animals following the templates. All the animals are made from 3 pieces and are sewn the same way. For each animal, cut 2 opposite shapes for the body and 1 for a gusset. The gusset shape is cut using the lower part of the animal pattern from the straight line downwards. If you place the folded fabric along the line and cut the lower body and legs double, it will open out into the full shape you need.

7 For each animal, match up one body half to the gusset, right sides together. Tack (baste) round the legs, joining the gusset to half of the body from gusset fold line at the back to the gusset fold line at the front. Stitch about 6 mm (¼ in) from the edge.

Join the second body side to the other half of the gusset with both sets of stitching meeting at the gusset fold line. Fold the stitched gusset with the right and left legs matching flat, so that you can stitch around the head and body, leaving a short length on the animal's back to turn it.

8 Turn the animal right side out and stuff it firmly, pushing the filling into the legs with a knitting needle or pencil. Oversew the opening to close it.

9 Make a paper pattern for Mr and Mrs Noah following the template. Cut 2 pieces of fabric for each figure, and join them by sewing around the outside edges with right sides together. With the points of the scissors, carefully make a small vertical slit in the back of each assembled figure and turn it to the right side. Stuff the figures firmly and oversew the openings. Make clothes by finishing squares and strips of fabric and sewing them in place.

THE NOAHS

ARK HULL

Picture **B**ricks

THIS ATTRACTIVE PUZZLE SETS A CHALLENGE FOR 1½ TO 3-YEAR-OLDS

YOU WILL NEED ■ *Sand paper* ■ *Length of pine, 5 × 5 cm (2 × 2 in),*
cut into squares ■ *Masking tape* ■ *Matt white emulsion (flat latex) paint* ■ *Paintbrushes* ■ *Pencil*
■ *Paper* ■ *Chalk* ■ *Non-toxic acrylic paints* ■ *Non-toxic clear acrylic varnish*

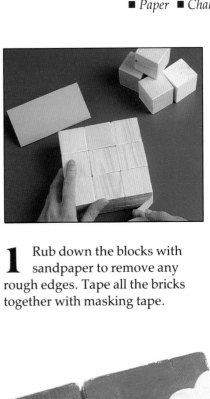

1 Rub down the blocks with sandpaper to remove any rough edges. Tape all the bricks together with masking tape.

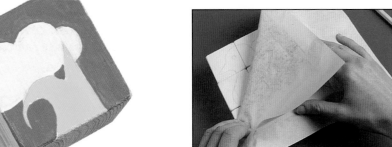

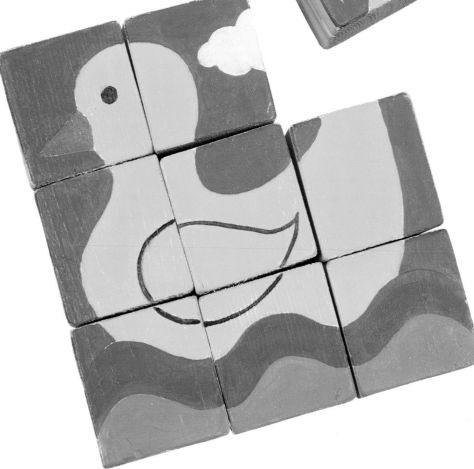

2 Prime the front with a coat of matt white emulsion (flat latex) paint. Draw out the picture of the duck onto a sheet of paper using the template as a guide, and then carefully transfer the picture, using a piece of chalk, onto the bricks.

3 Paint in the design. Leave the paint to dry and remove the masking tape. Cover with a coat of clear acrylic varnish.

Rotating **C**lown

NOW HAPPY, NOW SAD, THIS CARD PROVIDES INSTANT REACTIONS

YOU WILL NEED ■ *Pair of compasses* ■ *Pencil* ■ *White card* ■ *Ruler* ■ *Scissors* ■ *Craft knife*
■ *Non-toxic acrylic paints* ■ *Small paintbrush* ■ *Winged paperclip*

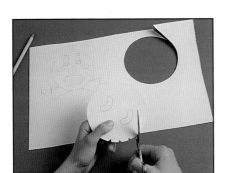

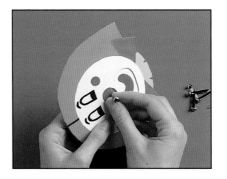

1 Use a pair of compasses to draw two circles, one slightly larger than the other, on a piece of white card. Mark the centres. The larger circle is the under piece which will be moved around. Scale up the templates and draw the two mouth shapes on the larger circle with a pencil.

The smaller circle is for the clown's face, so use the template to draw on the features, hair and bow tie. These must take up a larger area than the circle underneath to hide it, although you must leave a little showing below the bow tie for turning.

Cut out the two circles with scissors and cut triangles into the edge of the larger circle so that it can be easily gripped when being turned. Use a craft knife to cut out a hole for the mouth on the smaller circle.

2 Using a small paintbrush and acrylic paints, paint all the different areas of colour onto the cut out shapes. Leaving the face white, carefully paint the mouth, cheeks and nose red, paint the eyes with black, paint the bow tie blue and the hair orange. The circumference of the circle underneath should be painted in yellow as shown.

3 With the sharp end of a pair of scissors, make a small hole at the centre of each of the two circles marked earlier. Placing the clown's face on top of the piece with the mouths, push the winged paperclip through both holes and open up the clip at the back to secure it. Now move the circle underneath so that the clown has a happy face, then a sad face.

Goldilocks Play Panel

THIS WALL HANGING CAN BE USED TO TELL THE TRADITIONAL FAIRY TALE

YOU WILL NEED ■ *Tape measure* ■ *4 plain cotton fabrics for strips*
■ *Pen* ■ *Paper* ■ *Scissors* ■ *Assorted fabrics for appliqué designs and Goldilocks*
■ *Iron-on interfacing* ■ *Iron* ■ *Pins* ■ *Needle and thread* ■ *Velcro* ■ *Plain fabric for loops* ■ *Plain*
fabric for back ■ *Fur fabric for bears* ■ *Non-toxic, fire retardant polyester filling*
(batting) ■ *Yellow embroidery thread* ■ *Dark embroidery thread* ■ *2 poles*

1 The panel is made from 4 appliquéd strips joined together. The top strip should measure 26 × 48 cm (10¼ × 19 in). The 3 others should measure 17 × 48 cm (6¾ × 19 in). Cut templates for all the appliqué design shapes, scaling up 3 sizes of chairs, porridge bowls, spoons and beds. Choose fabrics carefully to show up the design, and cut them out using iron-on interfacing on easily frayed fabrics. Assemble the cut shapes on each strip, then pin and appliqué each one. Press all the appliqué work.

2 Pin the right sides of the strips together and stitch them in the correct order for the story. Sew small Velcro squares (using the hooked surface) to the path by the house, and on the cushions and beds.

3 Make 6 fabric loops each about 5 × 18 cm (2 × 7 in) in size. Fold in half and pin to the top and bottom of the hanging so that they are spaced evenly and can be incorporated into the final seam.

Cut a back piece the same size as the front, pin to the front with right sides together and then tack (baste) it in place. Stitch all round the hanging, sewing in the loops at top and bottom, and leaving a short length open on 1 side. Trim the seam edges. Turn right side out and press the seam, picking out the corners with a pin.

4 Make patterns for Goldilocks and the 3 bears, scaling the bears in size so they will fit their own chairs and beds. Cut Goldilocks from cotton fabric and the bears from fur fabric. Cut 2 shapes for each, sew them right sides together and cut a small slit in the back of each figure. Turn right side out, stuff and oversew the openings.

Sew yellow embroidery thread to Goldilocks for her hair and embroider dark eyes on the bears. Sew a square of Velcro to the back of each figure.

5 Cut coverlets for each bed and neaten the edges; they should be cut wide enough to go over their own bear. Stitch in a 'hinge' to the left side of each bed, and fix to the right with Velcro. Suspend the hanging from a pole threaded through the top loops, and add a bottom pole.

Asleep/Awake Bear

A DELIGHTFUL, TRADITIONAL CUDDLY TOY TO ENCOURAGE FIRST SPEECH

YOU WILL NEED ■ *Pen* ■ *Paper* ■ *Scissors* ■ *Corduroy or strong fabric* ■ *Tape measure* ■ *Needle and thread* ■ *2 safety eyes* ■ *Non-toxic, flame retardant polyester filling (batting)* ■ *Scraps of striped and patterned cotton fabric* ■ *Plain white cotton fabric* ■ *Iron* ■ *Pins* ■ *Embroidery thread*

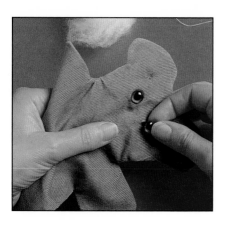

1 Make a paper pattern for the bear using the template as a guide. Cut 2 bear shapes from the corduroy fabric and make a 10 cm (4 in) vertical slit in the centre back of one of the shapes. Place the right sides together and tack (baste) in place before stitching all round, 6 mm (¼ in) from the edge. Carefully clip the main curves to give a smooth finish. Turn to the right side through the slit.

2 Mark positions for the eyes and attach them according to the manufacturer's instructions. Begin stuffing the bear, lightly filling both sets of ears and stitching diagonally across to give them shape. Ensure there is plenty of padding behind the eyes. After stuffing, oversew the back slit to close. Embroider the facial features and details onto the bears' heads and paws.

3 Cut a piece of patterned cotton for Awake Bear's dress 37 × 17 cm (14½ × 6¾ in) and a striped piece for the sleeping bag 37 × 13 cm (14½ × 5¼ in) with stripes running down the shorter side. Stitch the 2 pieces together along the longer edge with right sides facing and press. Cut a heart shape with the stripes running across and appliqué it to the centre of one side of the sleeping bag. Cut a strip of white cotton 37 × 10 cm (14½ × 4 in). Stitch this to the long side of the striped cotton. Press the seam away from the striped cotton and fold the white fabric to the wrong side leaving a 4 cm (1½ in) strip showing for Asleep Bear's sheet. Turn under the raw edge of the fabric and stitch it to the inside.

4 Stitch a 1 cm (³⁄₈ in) hem on the long raw edge of the dress section. Press. Make the piece into a tube by stitching the raw side edges together, matching hems and the ends of the seam. Half turn the tube along the centre seam with the wrong sides facing and press firmly.

5 Attach the sleeping bag to Asleep Bear by stitching the sheet section closed close to each side of the head and out to the sheet ends, ensuring that the heart shows on the centre front. Attach the dress top to Awake Bear by centring the dress and firmly stitching the dress back to the dress front, close to each side of the head. Also stitch the front to the back under the arms close to the body. By pulling the central hem up and down, the bears can be asleep or awake!

Hobby Horse

THIS TRADITIONAL HORSE MAKES A FRIENDLY TOY FOR AN OLDER CHILD

YOU WILL NEED ■ *Pencil* ■ *Paper* ■ *Scissors* ■ *Corduroy or strong cotton fabric*
■ *Patterned cotton fabric* ■ *Pins* ■ *Needle and strong thread* ■ *Iron* ■ *Card* ■ *Tape measure*
■ *Yarn* ■ *Non-toxic, flame retardant polyester filling (batting)* ■ *Safety eyes with moving centres*
■ *Embroidery thread* ■ *Plain fabric for reins and bridle* ■ *2 toy quality wooden rings*
■ *Sandpaper* ■ *Wooden broom-handle* ■ *Fretsaw (scroll saw)* ■ *2 toy bells*

1 Use the template as a guide and draw the head and ear pieces onto white paper and cut them out. Cut 2 shapes for the outer ears from the corduroy and 2 inner ears from the cotton fabric. Pin the right sides of each inner and outer ear piece together and tack (baste) then stitch them, leaving the bottom ends open. Turn out to the right side and press firmly.

Cut a strip of card about 9 cm (3½ in) wide and wind the yarn round it, cutting through the yarn at one side to form 18 cm (7 in) lengths for the mane.

2 Cut out the 2 head pieces from the corduroy or strong cotton fabric. Leaving the neck end open, pin and tack (baste) them, right sides together, around the front of the head and stop short just past the eye position. Enclose the centre of each strand of yarn into the seam as you tack (baste) down the back of the neck.

The mane must stop about 8 cm (3¼ in) short of the neck bottom. Do this firmly, strand by strand, so that it cannot be pulled out. Small children can be surprisingly forceful with their toys, so it is important to ensure that all the components are as securely attached as possible. Sew around the edges and remove the tacking (basting) threads. Stuff the 2 ears firmly with polyester filling (batting), and stitch the bottom ends to close.

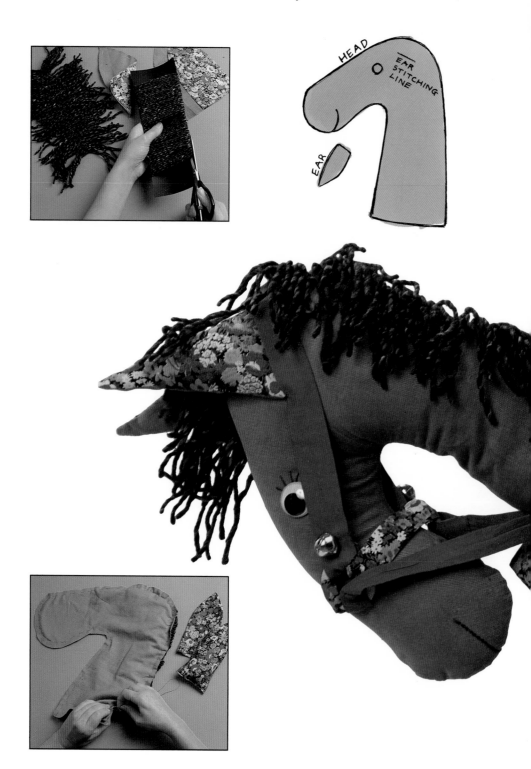

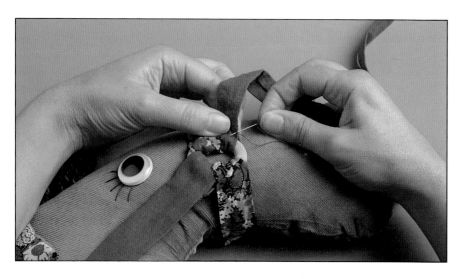

3 Clip the seam at the sharp inner neck curve and turn the head to the right side. Mark the positions for the eyes and attach them according to the manufacturer's instructions. Embroider the eyelashes. Sew a 1 cm (3/8 in) hem around the neck base. Attach the ears to the side of the head by stitching them firmly along the ear bottoms.

4 Stuff the head firmly at the top and down the neck but leave the bottom end of the neck loosely filled. Stitch the top backs of the ears to the head near the top so that they cannot flop. Make hemmed lengths of patterned and plain fabric for the bridle and reins and attach them securely using the wooden rings. Embroider the horse's mouth.

5 Sand down the broom-handle to remove any splinters. With a fretsaw (scroll saw), make a groove all round the handle, about 12 cm (4¾ in) from the end. Thread a needle with a long, double, strong cotton thread and wind the thread a few times around the groove. Push the grooved end of the handle into the neck and arrange the filling so the handle sits centrally inside the neck, stuffing it firmly. Ensure that you don't stuff the needle and thread in with it!

6 Gather the neck evenly round with one hand, about 6 cm (2¼ in) from the hem, and sew through to the outside. Wind the thread tightly round the gathers to catch them tightly, then pass the needle back and forth several times from one side of the neck to the other. Secure the thread firmly.

Make a further length of fabric to wind around the gathers of the neck. Make a bow to hide the threads and the stitching and stitch it down so it cannot be pulled off or be undone. Attach the 2 bells securely on either side of the bridle.

Pecking Woodpecker

PULL THE WOODPECKER TO THE TOP OF THE POLE, AND WATCH AS IT HOPS DOWN!

YOU WILL NEED ■ *Ruler* ■ *Pencil* ■ *Tracing paper* ■ *4 × 2.5 cm (1½ × 1 in)*
softwood, 1 cm (⅜ in) thick ■ *Fretsaw (scroll saw)* ■ *Hand drill* ■ *Coarse and fine sandpaper*
■ *35 cm (13½ in) dowelling, 8 mm (5/16 in) in diameter* ■ *10 × 10 cm (4 × 4 in) softwood, 3 cm (1¼ in) thick*
■ *3 × 2.5 cm (1¼ × 1 in) softwood, 2 cm (¾ in) thick* ■ *Medium-tension spring, 5 mm (3/16 in)*
in diameter ■ *Pliers* ■ *Non-toxic acrylic paints* ■ *Fine paintbrushes* ■ *Wood glue*

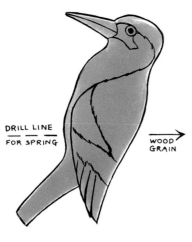

DRILL LINE FOR SPRING

WOOD GRAIN

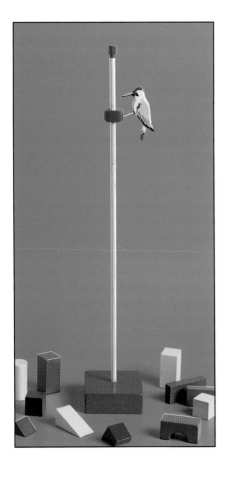

1 Scale up the template and trace onto the 1 cm (⅜ in) thick piece of softwood with the grain horizontal to the woodpecker. Cut out accurately with a fretsaw (scroll saw). Drill a 5 mm (3/16 in) hole 1 cm (2.5 cm) deep in the centre front of the woodpecker and sand to shape.

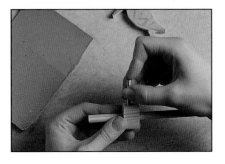

3 Slide the block onto the dowelling. Push one end of the spring into the small block and the other in the woodpecker. Rock the woodpecker, checking that it will cause the block to slide down the rod in a series of small jerks. If the steps are too big, slightly reduce the height of the block.

2 Sand the dowelling. Drill an 8 mm (5/16 in) hole, 2 cm (¾ in) deep in the centre of the square block and push in the dowelling. Take the softwood block and drill a 6 mm (¼ in) hole through the centre and a 5 mm (3/16 in) hole at right-angles to the large hole, to take one end of the spring. Sand the 6 mm (¼ in) hole until the block slides easily up and down the dowelling. If the spring is too long, trim it using pliers.

4 Take all the pieces apart and paint the components, but leave the dowelling and the inside of the sliding block unpainted. (The sanded hole will allow the woodpecker to slide up and down easily, but any paint in the hole will hinder this movement.) When the paint is dry, re-join the base and spring parts with a dab of glue, and fix a small block, cut from the woodpecker scrap, to the top of the dowelling.

Bird on a **S**tick

THIS BIRD MAKES AN ATTRACTIVE ORNAMENT FOR THE NURSERY

YOU WILL NEED ■ *White paper* ■ *Pencil* ■ *Piece of plywood,*
10 mm (3/8 in) thick ■ *Fretsaw (scroll saw)* ■ *Piece of thicker plywood* ■ *Ruler*
■ *Sandpaper* ■ *Drill* ■ *Wood glue* ■ *15 cm (6 in) length of dowelling* ■ *Paintbrushes*
■ *Non-toxic acrylic paints* ■ *Non-toxic clear acrylic varnish*

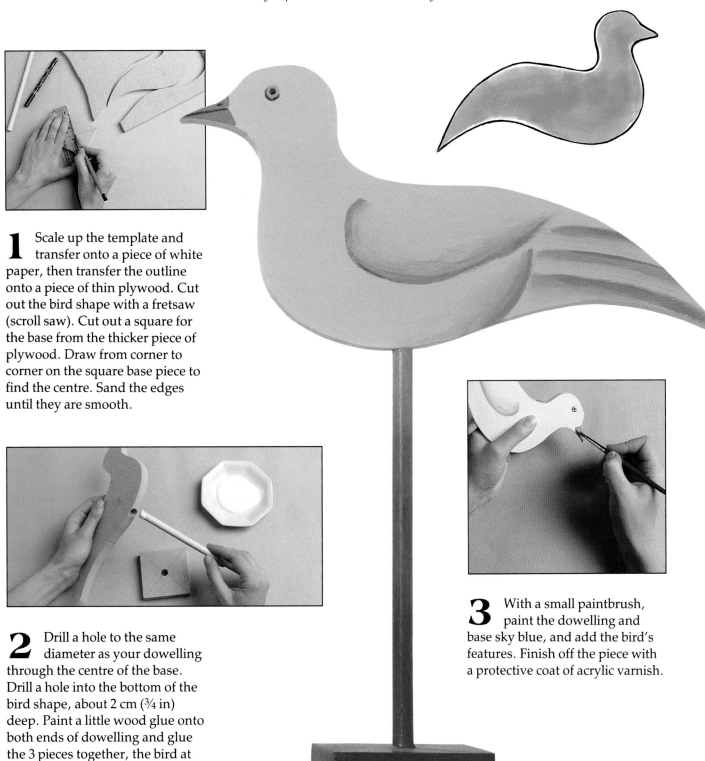

1 Scale up the template and transfer onto a piece of white paper, then transfer the outline onto a piece of thin plywood. Cut out the bird shape with a fretsaw (scroll saw). Cut out a square for the base from the thicker piece of plywood. Draw from corner to corner on the square base piece to find the centre. Sand the edges until they are smooth.

2 Drill a hole to the same diameter as your dowelling through the centre of the base. Drill a hole into the bottom of the bird shape, about 2 cm (3/4 in) deep. Paint a little wood glue onto both ends of dowelling and glue the 3 pieces together, the bird at one end and the base at the other.

3 With a small paintbrush, paint the dowelling and base sky blue, and add the bird's features. Finish off the piece with a protective coat of acrylic varnish.

Brick Town

THESE FUN HOUSES PROVIDE AN IMAGINATIVE BACKGROUND FOR OTHER TOYS

YOU WILL NEED ■ *Scrap wood* ■ *Pencil* ■ *Ruler* ■ *Saw* ■ *Sandpaper*
■ *Matt white emulsion (flat latex) paint* ■ *Enamel paints* ■ *Paintbrushes*

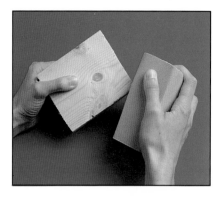

1 Ask your local wood yard for small pieces of scrap wood which are often free or sold at a cheaper rate. Pieces may already be the right size or you may have to cut them down with a saw. Use a ruler and a pencil to mark off the suitable lengths.

2 Smooth down all the edges and ends of each piece of wood with a sheet of sandpaper wrapped around a wooden block. Be sure to do this carefully, as pieces of scrap wood can be very rough both on the surface and the cut ends.

3 Paint the blocks of wood with a coat of white emulsion (flat latex) paint to seal them, and then paint on the house details and the hedges with enamel paints, following the manufacturer's instructions. Leave to dry thoroughly.

Clown Finger Puppets

THESE PUPPETS PROVIDE AN EASY WAY TO ENTERTAIN YOUR CHILDREN

YOU WILL NEED ■ *Pieces of felt in several colours* ■ *Scissors* ■ *Rubber-based glue*

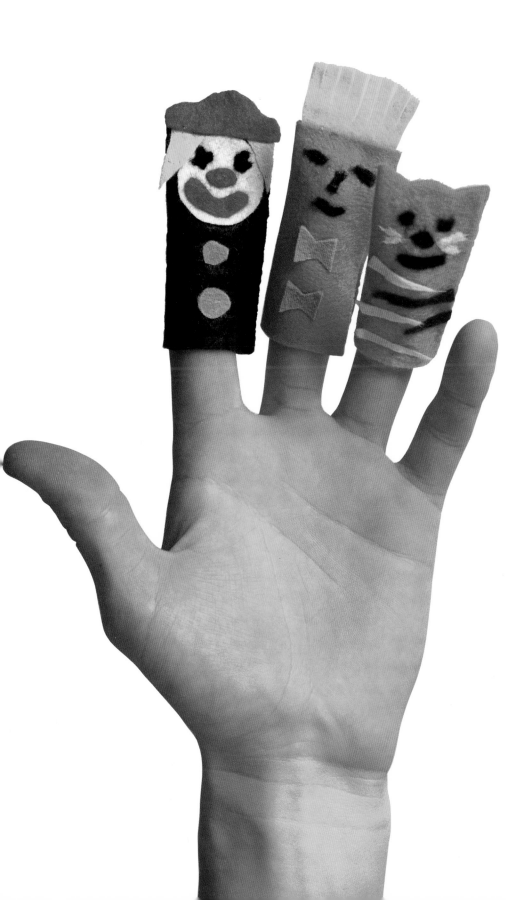

1 Cut out a rectangle of dark green felt which will fit around your finger for the body. Cut out all the other detail pieces: a face from white felt, two eyes from black felt, a nose, mouth and hat from red felt and two buttons from light green felt.

2 Fold the rectangular piece of felt in half and stick down the side and top edge with glue so that it fits onto your finger. Stick all the detailed features pieces onto this base piece. Leave the completed felt puppet under a heavy book for a couple of hours until the glue is completely dry. You can make other variations using the same methods.

Clapper

THIS TRADITIONAL WOODEN TOY IS SIMPLE TO MAKE BUT VERY EFFECTIVE

YOU WILL NEED ■ *Fretsaw (scroll saw)* ■ *36 × 4.5 cm (14 × 1¾ in) piece of wood, 1 cm (⅜ in) thick* ■ *Ruler* ■ *Pencil* ■ *Masking tape* ■ *Hand drill* ■ *Sandpaper* ■ *Scissors* ■ *Coloured card* ■ *Rubber-based glue* ■ *Length of cord*

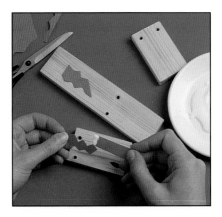

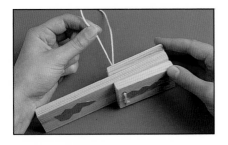

3 Tie all the pieces together with the cord, and knot securely. The cord should be just loose enough to allow the pieces to 'clap' together.

1 Cut 3 lengths of wood, one piece 18 cm (7 in) long and 2 pieces 8 cm (3¼ in) long. Secure the 3 pieces in position on top of each other with masking tape. Lining up one end, and with the longer piece sandwiched in the middle, drill 2 holes 1 cm (⅜ in) in from the inner corners, drilling through all 3 pieces of wood at once. Smooth down all the rough edges of the wood with sandpaper wrapped around a wooden block.

2 Cut out some decorative shapes from coloured card and glue onto the 'handle' and top piece of the clapper.

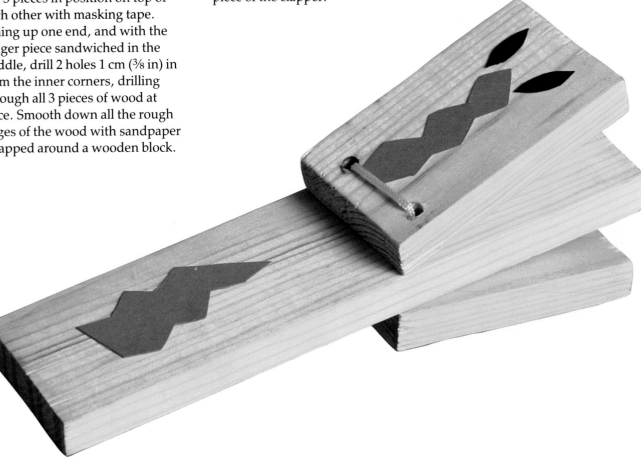

Fabric Book

TEXTURES, SOUNDS AND SHAPES ARE ALL STITCHED TOGETHER IN THIS BABY BOOK

YOU WILL NEED ■ *Tape measure* ■ *Ruler* ■ *Pencil* ■ *Scissors*
■ *Assorted washable fabrics such as fur fabric, vinyl, satin and bright plain and patterned cottons* ■ *Pins* ■ *Needle and thread* ■ *Iron* ■ *Embroidery threads* ■ *Washable satin ribbon in assorted colours* ■ *Toy bell* ■ *3 large buttons* ■ *Strong cotton thread*

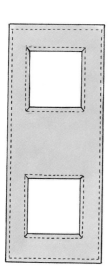

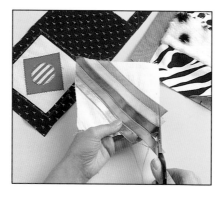

2 Cut some plain cotton slightly larger than the square hole and stitch the ribbons diagonally across it. Trim the ribbon edges and tack (baste) the square behind the hole. Prepare a design for the other side and stitch the two 'pictures' to the cover. Prepare an inside cover with different designs on each side. Remember that the spine section will require a strip 6 cm (2¼ in) wide that is free of design work.

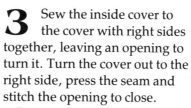

1 The book is made from a folded 'cover' which fastens along the spine to enclose a centre double-sided fabric page. The final arrangement of colours, patterns and textures on each page is up to you, but you could use different combinations of squares, circles, triangles and joined strips.

To assemble, cut pieces of fabric to the pattern dimensions given in the template. Cut out the central squares, clip into the corners and then turn 1 cm (⅜ in) under around the edges, tacking (basting) the hems in place.

3 Sew the inside cover to the cover with right sides together, leaving an opening to turn it. Turn the cover out to the right side, press the seam and stitch the opening to close.

Prepare the central page with a separate design each side leaving a 3 cm (1¼ in) strip on the spine side free of design work. Sew it together like a bag with the open end at the spine. A toy bell in a small cotton bag can be enclosed within the 2 layers of the page if you wish; this should be stitched through all the layers.

4 Fold the cover in half and insert the centre page. With doubled strong cotton thread, sew a button through from the front to the back so that all the layers are joined, and continue sewing the button until there is no possibility of its being pulled off. Sew on 2 more buttons and oversew the top edges of all the pages together at the spine, top and bottom, with the strong thread.

Leaf Counting Book

A BEAUTIFUL AND UNUSUAL CLOTH COUNTING BOOK

YOU WILL NEED ■ *3 sheets of plain paper* ■ *Pencil* ■ *3 pieces of 33 × 18 cm (13 × 7 in) calico (cotton fabric)* ■ *Pressed autumn leaves in different sizes* ■ *Rubber-based glue* ■ *Iron-on protective laminating film* ■ *Iron* ■ *Heat-resistant foam* ■ *Large darning needle* ■ *Length of fine cord* ■ *Metal ruler* ■ *Craft knife*

1 To work out how many leaves you will need for each page and how you will arrange them, make up a paper 'dummy' book. Fold each of the sheets of paper in half and put them together to make a 12-page 'book' Turn to the first page and draw a number 1 where you want to stick your first leaf. On the right-hand page draw the numbers 1 and 2. Turn over and draw the numbers 1 to 3 on the left-hand page and 1 to 4 on the right. Continue through the book until the last page is numbered 1 to 10.

2 Using the dummy book as a guide, open it at the centre. Lay out a piece of calico (cotton fabric) and arrange a pattern of 5 leaves on the left-hand side and 6 on the right-hand side, fixing each leaf by using a small piece of card to apply a dot of rubber-based glue on its reverse side. Press each leaf down lightly onto the calico (cotton fabric). It is important that you remember to leave a margin of about 12 mm (½ in) around the edges so that you can trim off the 'pages' neatly when you have finished the book.

3 Cut 6 pieces, about 33 × 19 cm (13 × 7½ in), from the protective laminating film. Carefully smooth one sheet over the leaves on the page so that it adheres lightly. Turn the sheet of calico (cotton fabric) over. Do the same with the centre page of the dummy. Arrange 7 leaves on left, and 4 on right. Cover this side with another sheet of film. Discard the dummy pages. Repeat with the other pieces of calico (cotton fabric), laying out the leaves as shown. Arrange a pretty pattern of leaves on the front cover.

4 Lay each sheet of calico (cotton fabric) on an ironing board and cover with heat resistant foam. Use your iron to seal the laminate. While still warm, fold the calico (cotton fabric) in half, in the same order as the dummy. Pierce 3 holes in the spine of each page and lace with cord. Trim the rough edges of the completed book.

Pop-Up Puppet

GIVE CHILDREN HOURS OF FUN WITH THIS DISAPPEARING PUPPET

YOU WILL NEED ■ *White paper* ■ *Pencil* ■ *Card* ■ *Piece of fabric* ■ *Scissors*
■ *Rubber-based glue* ■ *Craft knife* ■ *Large hollow rubber ball* ■ *30 cm (12 in) length of dowelling*
■ *Ribbon* ■ *Needle and thread* ■ *Black felt-tip pen*

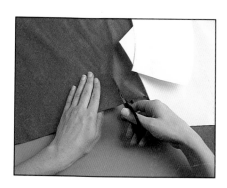

1 Scale up the templates shown and cut out a piece of card using the card template. Using the fabric template, cut out the fabric with a sharp pair of scissors.

2 Next fold the piece of card into a cone shape and stick down the edges with glue so that it stays in shape. When the glue is dry, stick the fabric onto the cone leaving a piece of fabric loose at the top end of the cone. At the smaller end snip into the fabric with a pair of scissors so that it can be folded easily into the inside of the cone and glued down.

3 Using a craft knife, cut a small cross into the ball and push the piece of dowelling in through the hole. Secure with a little glue, then place the dowelling through the cone with the ball at the top.

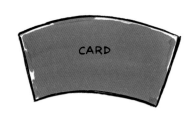

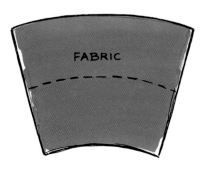

CARD

FABRIC

4 Secure the loose fabric to the dowelling with glue and a ribbon tied in a bow just below the ball. To make the bow safe, sew a couple of stitches through it. Draw on the eyes, nose and mouth with a black felt-tip pen. Pull the dowelling up and down through the cone to make the puppet's head pop up and down.

Play Dough

STORE PLAY DOUGH IN A PLASTIC CONTAINER WITH AN AIRTIGHT LID

YOU WILL NEED ■ *225 g/8 oz/2 cups plain (all-purpose) flour* ■ *115 g/4 oz/1 cup salt*
■ *2 tsp cream of tartar* ■ *Mixing bowl* ■ *Spoon* ■ *Thick-bottomed saucepan* ■ *2 tbsp oil* ■ *10 fl oz/*
½ pt/2 cups water ■ *Food colouring* ■ *Vanilla essence (extract) for fragrance* ■ *Pastry board*

1 Measure out the dry ingredients into a large mixing bowl and then stir them together thoroughly.

2 Put the dry ingredients in the saucepan with the oil, water, colouring and vanilla essence (extract) and stir continuously over a low heat until a dough forms.

3 Turn the dough out onto a lightly floured pastry board and knead while the mixture cools. Continue to knead for 5–10 minutes. If the mixture is too dry, occasionally dampen your hands while kneading, and if it is too sticky, dust with a little extra flour.

82

Sunshine T-Shirt

BRIGHTEN UP A PLAIN WHITE T-SHIRT WITH THIS SMILING SUN

YOU WILL NEED ■ *Pencil* ■ *Card* ■ *Scissors* ■ *T-shirt* ■ *Iron* ■ *Paintbrushes*
■ *Yellow, red and gold fabric paints* ■ *Black fabric pen*

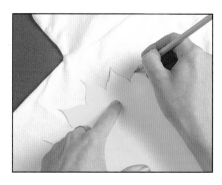

1 Scale up the template onto a piece of card and cut it out. Press the T-shirt, then lay it out on a flat surface and place some card inside to protect the back from paint. Position the template on the front side of the T-shirt and draw around the edge in pencil to transfer the design.

2 Using a small paintbrush and yellow fabric paint, colour in the sun shape.

3 Mix a little red paint with some yellow and blend into the rays. Add some gold around the edges and enhance the circle around the face. When dry, use the black fabric pen to draw on the eyes, nose and mouth and outline the whole sun to give a bolder effect. Iron the shirt carefully to fix the paint according to the manufacturer's instructions, and wash before use.

French Knot Smock

AN ADAPTABLE DRESS WHICH SUITS ALL SHAPES AND SIZES

YOU WILL NEED ■ *Tape measure* ■ *Pen* ■ *Paper* ■ *Scissors* ■ *Washable cotton velvet* ■ *Wadding (batting)* ■ *Pins* ■ *Needle and thread* ■ *Iron* ■ *Bias binding or patterned fabric* ■ *Zip (zipper)* ■ *Embroidery thread* ■ *Hook and eye fastening*

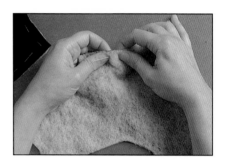

1 This design can be adapted to fit any age or size. Scale up the template according to the size you require and make a paper pattern for the bodice. The skirt width must be calculated to include gathering and will vary according to your fabric, but looks prettiest when it is quite full. Cut out 2 opposite bodice backs and a front from the velvet and the wadding (batting). Tack (baste) the wadding (batting) to the wrong side of the velvet.

2 Pin, tack (baste) and sew the bodice sections right sides together at the shoulder seams. Press the seams open with a cool iron. Tack (baste) the back opening edges down 1 cm (⅜ in) and press flat.

3 Cut the bodice linings from patterned fabric. Join the shoulders right sides together and press the seams open.

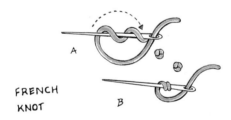

FRENCH KNOT

PLACE TO FOLD

4 Cut the skirt in 1 piece and tack (baste) the back seam closed leaving sufficient open at the top end for the zip (zipper). Stitch the seam and neaten the raw edges. Gather the skirt around the waist, draw up the gathers and pin to the bodice right sides together, adjusting the gathers evenly to fit.

Tack (baste) the bodice to the skirt, taking a 1 cm (⅜ in) seam allowance, lining up the tacked-(basted-)down bodice opening and the neatened back seam of the skirt. Stitch the skirt to the bodice, trim and oversew the raw edges. Turn right side out and pin, tack (baste) and sew the zip (zipper) into the back opening.

5 Matching shoulder seams, pin the bodice lining to the dress, wrong sides together. Turn the back lining openings under and tack (baste) them to the back seam allowance. Tack (baste) the lining to the bodice around the neck and armholes. Hem the lining to the back openings.

Concealing all the raw edges at the top back opening, pin, tack (baste) and sew bias binding or strips of patterned fabric right sides together around the neck about 1 cm ($\frac{3}{8}$ in) from the edge. Turn to the wrong side and hem the binding neatly under, catching it to the lining. Work the armholes in the same way. Hem the bottom of the lining to the dress/bodice seam allowance.

6 Using 3 strands of embroidery thread, decorate the bodice by stitching French knots to join the lining to the bodice through the wadding (batting). Use the patterned lining to guide you in placing your knots evenly. Backstitch the thread on the inside to secure it, take the needle to the outside and sew the knot before returning the needle through to the lining at exactly the same point. Secure the thread and cut. Continue to complete the bodice backs and fronts. Sew a hook and eye to the bodice opening, and hem the skirt.

85

Baseball Cap

THE PERFECT HEAD-GEAR FOR A STAR-STRUCK TODDLER

YOU WILL NEED ■ *Pencil* ■ *Stiff card* ■ *Scissors* ■ *Blue and yellow felt*
■ *Baseball cap* ■ *Pins* ■ *Rubber-based glue*

1 Draw the star shapes onto a piece of card. Cut 2 stars from the card, one large size and one small. Place the small template on the blue felt, draw round with a pencil and cut out 4 stars. In the same way, using the large template, cut out 4 stars from the yellow felt.

2 Arrange the stars across the front of the cap. When you are satisfied with the positions, pin in place. Stick down the stars, ensuring that the glue covers the felt right to the point.

Earflap Hat

THIS STRIPY HAT WITH ITS BRIGHT TASSELS FITS 1 TO 3-YEAR-OLDS

YOU WILL NEED ■ *Small quantity of double knitting (sport) yarn in each of the following colours: Yellow – A; Cerise – B; Orange – C; Turquoise – D; Lime – E; Pink – F; Red – G; Blue – H; Purple – I* ■ *1 pair of 4 mm (US 5) knitting needles* ■ *Tape measure* ■ *Scissors* ■ *Brush*

Tension (Gauge)
Using 4 mm (US 5) needles, 20 sts and 26 rows to 10 cm (4 in) (st st).

HAT
Cast on 72 sts using yarn A. Work 6 rows garter st (every row k). Continue in st st (1 row k, 1 row p) for 46 rows in the following colour sequence: (4 rows B, 6 rows C, 8 rows D, 4 rows E, 8 rows F, 6 rows G, 4 rows A, 6 rows H).
Inc row: *k 7, k into front and back of next st. Repeat from * to end.
Next row and every even numbered row: p to end.
Inc row: * k 8, k into front and back of next st. Repeat from * to end of row.
Continue in this way, increasing 9 sts every alternate row until *k 13, k into front and back of next st. Repeat from * to end (135 sts). Work 4 rows without shaping.
Dec row: *k 13, k 2 tog. Repeat from * to end.
Next row and every even numbered row: p to end.
Dec row: *k 12, k 2 tog. Repeat from * to end.
Continue decreasing in this way on every odd numbered row until 9 sts remain.
Break yarn, thread end through sts, draw up and sew seam.

EARFLAPS
(Make 1 in yarn E and 1 in yarn I)
With right side facing, pick up 18 sts (7 sts from back of head seam) along cast-on edge of hat. Work 4 rows garter stitch (every row k).
5th row: k 2 tog, k 14, k 2 tog.
Next 3 rows: k to end.
9th row: k 2 tog, k 12, k 2 tog.
Next 3 rows: k to end.

13th row: k 2 tog, k 10, k 2 tog.
Next 2 rows: k to end.
16th row: k 2 tog, k 8, k 2 tog.
17th row: k to end.
18th row: k 2 tog, k 6, k 2 tog (8 sts).
Cast (bind) off.

Toggle
Using yarn C, cast on 7 sts.
Next row: cast (bind) off 7 sts.
Attach toggle to centre of hat.

Braided cords
Cut 3 strands of different coloured yarn 58 cm (23 in) long. Thread the strands through centre of cast-off (bound-off) edge on earflaps. Braid the 6 strands, keeping like colours together, and knot the end leaving 6 cm (2¼ in) of spare yarn with which to make the tassel.

Tassel
Cut several different coloured strands of yarn, 12 cm (4¾ in) long. Tie a length of yarn tightly around the centre of the strands. Place the knot of the braid in the centre of the strands and tie firmly into place. Brush the tassel to separate the strands and trim the ends neatly.

Starfish T-Shirt

THIS DETACHABLE STARFISH ACTS AS BOTH MOTIF AND FUN TOY

YOU WILL NEED ■ *Marker pen* ■ *White paper* ■ *Scissors*
■ *Felt in 2 contrasting colours* ■ *Embroidery thread* ■ *Needle and thread* ■ *20 cm (8 in) Velcro*
■ *Wadding (batting)* ■ *Pins* ■ *Pinking shears* ■ *T-shirt*

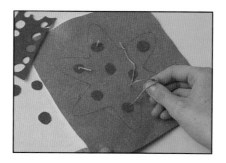

1 Use the marker pen to draw a starfish shape on a piece of white paper. Cut it out and draw around it on 2 pieces of felt.

2 Cut out some dots in a different coloured felt and attach securely with embroidery thread on one of the stars.

3 Sew 1 piece of Velcro to the middle of the other piece of felt, and another to the front of the T-shirt.

4 Sandwich a piece of wadding (batting) between the 2 felt layers, pin together and sew around the starfish shape.

5 Using pinking shears, cut out the starfish shape just outside the stitching line, and attach to the T-shirt.

Pig T-Shirt

THIS MOTIF CAN BE SCALED UP TO FIT ANY SIZE OF T-SHIRT

YOU WILL NEED ■ *White paper* ■ *Black felt-tip pen* ■ *White T-shirt* ■ *Pencil* ■ *White card* ■ *Fine black fabric pen* ■ *Pink fabric pen* ■ *Grey yarn* ■ *Scissors* ■ *Large darning needle* ■ *Iron*

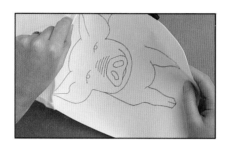

1 Scale up the pig template and draw the outline onto white paper using a black pen. Slip the paper inside the T-shirt so the design can be seen through the fabric. Draw the outline onto the T-shirt in pencil. Remove the drawing and replace it with the piece of white card inside the T-shirt beneath the pencil drawing. This will give a firm base when you use the fabric pen and will also prevent the ink from bleeding through to the back.

2 Start drawing with the black fabric pen. Fill in the eyes and colour the snout using the pink fabric pen.

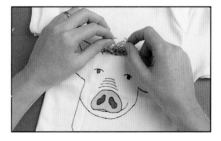

3 Cut some grey yarn into short lengths and use the darning needle to sew them onto the head of the pig. Separate the strands to fluff out the 'hair' and make it look realistic.

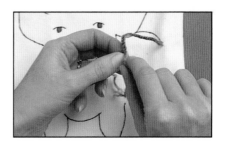

4 Sew 3 long lengths of yarn onto the rear of the pig. Braid the strands, tie into a knot at the end and trim. Press the design on the inside of the T-shirt to fix the fabric colours, according to the manufacturer's instructions.

Reversible Sun Hat

TWO HATS IN ONE FOR BABIES OF 5 TO 12 MONTHS

YOU WILL NEED ■ *Tracing paper* ■ *Pencil* ■ *Ruler*
■ *White paper* ■ *Pins* ■ *Scissors* ■ *23 × 115 cm (9 × 45 in) red striped fabric* ■ *23 × 115 cm*
(9 × 45 in) green striped fabric ■ *Needle and thread* ■ *Iron*

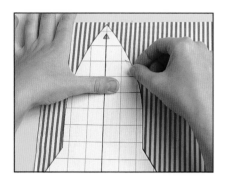

1 Scale up the template onto white paper to the required size and cut out. A 1 cm (⅜ in) seam allowance is included on all template edges. Pin the pattern to the fabric and cut out 6 pieces in each colour.

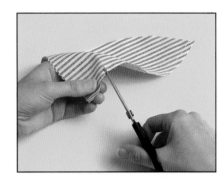

2 Working with one colour at a time, take 2 panels and pin them with right sides together. Sew from the top point along the edge to the brim edge. Snip the seam allowance as marked on the template. Press the seam open.

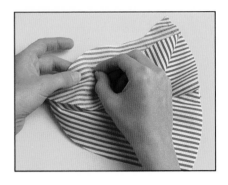

3 Pin on a third panel. Sew from the top point to the brim edge, snip and press seam open. Repeat these stages with the remaining 3 panels so that you have 2 separate 3-panel pieces. Repeat with the other colour.

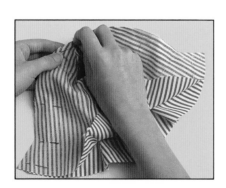

4 Now pin both made-up sections of one colour with right sides together. Match top points and brim edges. Sew from one brim edge, up and over the top points, and down to the other brim edge. Snip as marked and press the seam open. Do the same for the other colour, so that you have 2 separate hats ready to join.

5 Place one hat inside the other with right sides together. Pin in position, carefully matching all the seams. Sew all the way around the outer brim edge, leaving a 7 cm (2¾ in) opening.

Turn the hat by reaching inside the opening, grasping the right side of the hat and pulling it out. Close the opening by turning the 1 cm (⅜ in) seam into the hat and tacking (basting) the edges together. Top stitch right around the outer brim edge. Remove the tacking (basting) threads.

SNIP HERE

SNIP HERE

Bright **S**weater

THIS EYE-CATCHING SWEATER IS GIVEN IN 2 SIZES – 6–12 MONTHS AND 2–3 YEARS

YOU WILL NEED ■ *Double knitting (sport) cotton in the quantities given below*
for each colour: 50 g (2-ounce skein) yellow – A; 50 g (2-ounce skein) lime – B; 100 g (4-ounce
skein) red – C; 50 g (2-ounce skein) orange – D; 100 g (4-ounce skein) pink – E; 50 g (2-ounce skein)
turquoise – F; 50 g (2-ounce skein) purple – G ■ *1 pair size 4 mm (US 5) knitting needles* ■ *1 pair*
size 3.5 mm (US 4) knitting needles ■ *Iron* ■ *Large darning needle* ■ *Tape measure*

Tension (Gauge)
Using 4 mm (US 5) needles, 20 sts
and 26 rows to 10 cm (4 in) (st st).

FRONT
Begin at the front neck edge.
Using 4 mm (US 5) needles and
yarn A, cast on 60(68) sts. Work
8 rows st st (1 row k, 1 row p).

Picot
K 17(19), (ynfwd, k 2 tog) to last
17(19) sts, k 17(19). Beginning with
a p row, work 3 rows st st. Join in
yarn B and continue with the
pattern as follows:
1st row: (k 2 in B, k 2 in A) to end
of row.
2nd row: (p 2 in A, p 2 in B) to end.
3rd row: (k 2 in A, k 2 in B) to end.
4th row: (p 2 in B, p 2 in A) to end.
Using yarn A work 2 rows st st.
Break cotton. Join in cotton C and
work 36(48) rows st st.

To shape sides
Inc 1 st at each end of next and
every following 8th row 3(4)
times more (68(78) sts).
Next row: p to end.

Ruffle
Inc row: using yarn A inc in every
st (k into front and back of each st)
(136(158) sts). Beginning with a p
row, work 9(11) rows st st. For the
picot, k 1 (ynfwd, k 2 tog) to last
st, k 1. Beginning with a p row
work 5 rows st st. Cast (bind) off.

BACK
Work same as the front, changing
the colours as follows.

Use D in place of A, A in place of
B, E in place of C.

SLEEVES
Using 4 mm (US 5) needles and
yarn F (G for second sleeve) cast
on 34(36) sts. To shape the sides,
inc 1 st at each end of 5th and
every following 5th row until
56(62) sts and 55(65) rows are
completed. Work 2 rows st st
without shaping. Cast (bind) off.

Wrist ruffles
(Knit 2 alike)
With the right side facing and
using 4 mm (US 5) needles and
yarn G, pick up 34(36) sts from the
cast-on edge of the sleeve.
Dec row: (k 1, k 2 tog) to end
(23(24) sts).
Next row: p to end.
Inc row: double sts (k into front
and back of each st) (46(48) sts).
Beginning with a p row work 5(7)
rows st st.

Picot
K 1, (ynfwd, k 2 tog) to last st, k 1.
Work 3 rows st st and then cast
(bind) off.

Bobbles
For flowers: make 4 in yarn E and
1 in yarn B.
For buttons: make 2 in yarn A.

Using 3.5 mm (US 4) needles,
cast on 3 sts.
Inc row: k into front and back of
each st (6 sts). Beginning with a
p row, work 5 rows st st.
Dec row: (k 2 tog) 3 times (3 sts).

Dec row: p 3 tog. Break yarn, thread end through remaining st. Run a gathering thread around edge, draw up to form bobble and secure.

TO MAKE UP

Press all pieces on the wrong side under a damp cloth. Fold under neck edge on picot and hem cast-on edge to wrong side of row. Fold under ruffle edge on picot and hem cast-off (bound-off) edge to inside of work. Join shoulder seams up to picot.

Place a marker 15(16) cm (6(6½) in) below shoulder seam on back and front for sleeve position. Sew the top of the sleeve between the markers using backstitch. Fold under the ruffle edge at the cuff on the picot and hem cast-off (bound-off) edge to wrong side of work. Join sleeve and side seams.

To make the buttonhole loops, use yarn D to make a small loop each side of the shoulder seam. Blanket stitch around the edge of the loop. Secure into place. Sew the bobbles to the front of the work to correspond with the loops. For the flower, sew the green bobble to centre front (10 rows above the ruffle). Sew on the pink bobbles to form the petals.

Tickle Mitts

JAZZ UP A SIMPLE PAIR OF BABY MITTS BY ADDING A BRIGHT FRINGE

YOU WILL NEED ■ *1 pair of 3.5 mm (US 4) knitting needles*
■ *25 g (1-ounce skein) blue 4-ply yarn* ■ *Tape measure* ■ *Large darning needle* ■ *Scissors*
■ *Small amount of bright pink double knitting (sport) yarn*

Tension (Gauge)
Using 3.5 mm (US 4) needles, 22 sts and 28 rows to 10 cm (4 in) (st st).

MITTS
(Knit 2 alike)
Using 3.5 mm (US 4) needles, cast on 32 sts and work 12 rows in k 1, p 1 rib.
Next row (lace hole row): (k 2, ynfwd, k 2 tog) 8 times.
Work straight in st st, starting with a p row, until mitt measures 10 cm (4 in), ending with a p row.

Shape top as follows
1st row: (k 1, k 2 tog through back of loop, k 10, k 2 tog, k 1) twice.
2nd and 4th rows: p to end.
3rd row: (k 1, k 2 tog through back of loops, k 8, k 2 tog, k 1) twice.
5th row: (k 1, k 2 tog through back of loops, k 6, k 2 tog, k 1) twice. Cast (bind) off on a knit row.

TO MAKE UP
Fold mitt in half (right sides together) and sew up side seam leaving end of mitt open. Cut 10 lengths of the bright pink yarn and taking 2 strands at a time, knot along end of mitt (joining open end of mitt at the same time) to form a fringe. Trim fringe to the length required. Repeat this with the other mitt. Finally, using 3 strands of bright pink yarn, make 2 braids, each 32 cm (12½ in) long, and thread them through the lace holes on each mitt.

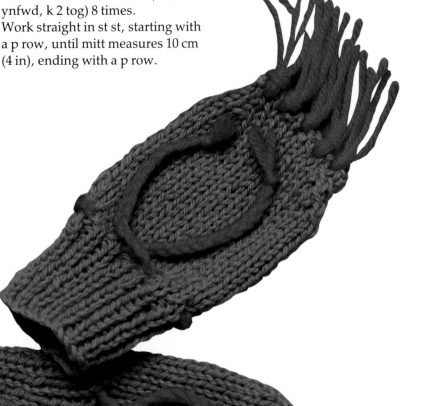

Stockists and Suppliers

FABRICS, SEWING, QUILTING AND HABERDASHERY SUPPLIES

The Cotton Club
Coxeter House
21–27 Ock Street
Abingdon
OX14 5AJ
UK
(0235) 550067

The Cotton Club
1 Rosemary Lane
Bampton
Oxon
OX8 2JJ
UK
(0993) 851234
(*Natural dress fabrics*)

DMC Creative World
Pullman Road
Wigston
Leicester
LE18 2DY
UK
(*Threads and cottons*)

Magpie Patchworks
Department G
37 Palfrey Road
Northbourne
Bournemouth
Dorset
BH10 6DN
UK

Mulberry Silks
2 Old Rectory Cottage
Easton Grey
Malmesbury
Wiltshire
SN16 0PE
UK
(0666) 840881

Patchworks and Quilts
9 West Place
Wimbledon
London
SW19 4UH
UK
(*Quilts and Fabrics*)

Quilt Basics
2 Meades Lane
Chesham
Bucks
HP5 1ND
UK

The Quilt Room
20 West Street
Dorking
Surrey
RH4 1BL
UK

Silken Strands
33 Linksway
Gatley
Cheadle
Cheshire
SK8 4LA
UK
(*Embroidery requisites*)

Strawberry Fayre
Chagford
Devon
TQ13 8EN
UK
(*Mail order fabrics*)

Threadbear Supplies
11 Northway
Deanshanger
Milton Keynes
MK19 6NF
UK
(*Waddings/battings*)

George Weil & Sons Ltd
The Warehouse
Reading Arch Road
Redhill
Surrey
RH1 1HG
UK
(0737) 778868
(*Fabric paints and equipment. Shop, mail order and export*)

DMC Corporation
Port Kearney
Building 10
South Kearney
New Jersey 07032–4688
USA
(*Threads and cottons*)

P & B Fabrics
898 Mahler Road
Burlingame
California 94010
USA

DMC Needlecraft Ltd
PO Box 317
Earlswood
NSW 2206
Australia

Auckland Folk Art Centre
591 Remuera Road
Remuera
Auckland
New Zealand
(09) 524 0936

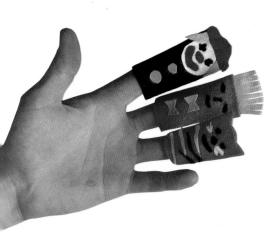

Quilt Connection Ltd
214 Nights Road
Lower Hutt
New Zealand
(04) 569 3427

Faysons Art Needlework Centre
135a Greenway
Box 84036
Greenside
Johannesburg
South Africa
(11) 646 0642

**KNITTING AND CROCHET
YARN SUPPLIES**

Arnotts
Argyle Street
Glasgow
UK
(041) 248 2951

Rowan Yarns
Green Lane Mill
Holmfirth
West Yorkshire
UK
(0484) 681881

Christa's Ball & Skein
971 Lexington Avenue No.1A
New York
New York 10021
USA
(212) 772 6960

Greenwich Yarns
2073 Greenwich Street
San Francisco 94123
USA
(415) 567 2535

Hook 'N' Needle
1869 Post Road East
Westport
Connecticut 06880
USA
(203) 259 5119

The London Knitting Company
2531 Rocky Ridge Road No.101
Birmingham
Alabama 35243
USA
(205) 822 5855

Westminster Trading Corporation
5 Northern Boulevard
Amherst
New Hampshire 03031
USA
(803) 886 5041
(*Yarn by mail order*)

A Knit Above
2427 Granville Street
Vancouver
V6H 3G5
Canada
(604) 734 0975

Imagiknit
2586 Yonge Street
Toronto
M4P 2J3
Canada
(416) 482 5287

Indigo Inc
155 Rue St Paul
Quebec City
G1K 3W2
Canada
(418) 694 1419

Greta's Handcrafts Centre
25 Lindfield Avenue
Lindfield
NSW 2070
Australia
(02) 416 2488

Mateira
250 Park Street
Victoria 3205
Australia
(03) 690 7651

Pots 'N' Stitches
113 London Circuit
ACT 2600
Australia
(062) 487 563

Randburg Needlework
19 Centre Point
Hill Street
Randburg
South Africa
(11) 787 3307

**ART SUPPLIES AND SPECIALIST
PAPERS**

Daler-Rowney Ltd
PO Box 10
Bracknell
Berkshire
RG12 8ST
UK
(0344) 424621
(*Paint specialists*)

One Four Nine Paper Supplies
PO Box A13
Huddersfield
West Yorkshire
HD3 4LW
UK
(*Mail order specialist*)

Paperchase
213 Tottenham Court
Road London
W1A 4US
(071) 580 8496